# A Portrait

# of

# Highcliffe

This new edition published by
Natula Publications
5 St Margarets Avenue, Christchurch, Dorset. BH23 1JD
www.natula.co.uk

Acknowledgments

The publishers would like to thank the following for the additional information and
the use of illustrations in this amended edition: -

Mr. Gurth Brooke
Mrs. Sally Glennie
Mrs. Olive J. Samuel

# MY THANKS

I am grateful to so many people for their knowledge of Highcliffe past and present, without whom this book would not have been possible.

To .....

Mrs. M.R.G. Alldridge
Miss Astridge
Rev. Gregory Carter
Dr. E.T. Brooks
Mr. L. Durrant
Elliott & Green
Miss M. Ellwood
Mr. & Mrs. Fagan
Mr. & Mrs. D. Frampton
Sister W. Giles
Mr. D. Grainger
Mr. H. Lee
Mrs. Little
Mrs. Lunn
Mr. & Mrs. J. Macfadyen
Mr. Pelly
Mr. D. Pratley & Mr. G. Millward of the Christchurch Borough Planning Dept.
Mr. T. Ramm
Miss A Rhymes
Mr. A.W. Robins
Rev. J. Seaford
Miss A. Sque
Mr. L. Strickland
Mr. & Mrs. Windust
Mrs. Withers
..... and many others who have provided information or vital clues.

A special word of thanks to Jane Martin of Natula Publications for all her help and advice.

Also to .....

Miss Jean Lunn for the sketch of La Grande Maison des Andelys.
Mr. Roland Adams for the photographs of Highcliffe Castle.
Mr. Jim Hunter and Mr. John Lewis at the Red House Museum, Christchurch, for the photographs of the houses: Belvedere, Hoburne, Chewton Mill, Culmore, Wolhayes, Holmhurst, Highcliffe Castle and beach.

# CONTENTS

Page

Chapter One      The Beginnings                                        1

Chapter Two      High Cliff                                           5

Chapter Three    Owners of the Highcliffe Estate                     11

Chapter Four     Highcliffe Castle I                                 16

Chapter Five     Country Houses                                      33

Chapter Six      The Churches                                        53

Chapter Seven    St Mark's Junior Mixed School 1844 - 1900           68

Chapter Eight    The Schools                                         79

Chapter Nine     The Village in the Nineteenth Century               87

Chapter Ten      The Village in the Twentieth Century                94

Chapter Eleven   Highcliffe Castle II                               111

Chapter Twelve   The Village 1970 - 2003                            117

Chapter Thirteen Reminiscences                                      123

Appendix A       Officiating Clergy of the Village of Highcliffe    130

Appendix B       General Practitioners Practising in Highcliffe     132

Appendix C       Staff of St. Mark's Church of England School       133

Appendix C       Staff of Highcliffe Junior School                  134

Appendix D       Road Names                                         136

                 Bibliography                                       138

# ILLUSTRATIONS

Page

Chapter One     'Little Megs'     2
Sea Corner     3
High Cliff     4
Chapter Two     Louisa, Marchioness of Waterford     6
Statue of Louisa, Marchioness of Waterford     9
Genealogy of the Owners of Highcliffe Castle     10
Chapter Three     Bure Hommage     11
Highcliffe Castle c.1950     14
Highcliffe Castle     15
Chapter Four     Oriel Window     17
Great Hall showing Jesse Window     19
La Grande Maison de Andelys     20
The Dining Room     21
The Drawing Room     22
The Great Hall     23
The Chapel     24
Plan of Highcliffe Castle     25
Queen Mary at Highcliffe Castle     32
Chapter Five     Hoburne House     33
'Domesday Oak'     34
Saulfland     35
Shelley Hill     36
Cranemoor House     37
Latimers     38
Nea House     39
Holmhurst     40
Belvedere     42
Wolhayes     43
Beacon Lodge     44
Culmore House     45
Greystones     46
Mountjoy     47
The Hoy     48
Chewton Mill     49
Amberwood     50

# ILLUSTRATIONS (Continued)

Page

Chapter Six       Highcliffe Church Restoration Account              55
                  Highcliffe Church Restoration - Labour Account     56
                  Club Accounts                                      59
                  St. Mark's Church                                  62
                  Highcliffe Methodist Church                        63
                  The Church of the Holy Redeemer                    65
                  Cranemoor Chapel                                   67
                  Highcliffe National Schools – Annual Balance       71
Chapter Seven     St. Mark's School                                 74
Chapter Eight     St. Mark's Church School                          81
Chapter Nine      Frampton's in Lymington Road                      89
                  Main Street, Highcliffe                            92
                  Shops in Lymington Road, opposite Post Office      93
Chapter Ten       The Village High Cliffe                           94
                  The Inauguration of Highcliffe Golf Course 1927    96
                  Highcliffe Hotel                                   97
                  Tea House c.1926                                   98
                  Highcliffe Amateur Dramatic Society                99
                  Radome at Steamer Point                           101
                  Adverts from Parish Magazine 1888                 106
Chapter Eleven    Highcliffe Castle before Restoration              111
                  Highcliffe Castle during Restoration              114
                  Restored Grand Portico                            115
Chapter Twelve    Heila House                                       118
                  Crows Nest Café                                   119
                  The Globe Highcliffe c.1908                       120
                  Stuart Lodge Hotel                                122
Reminiscences     Sea Corner (Now G & T's)                         123
                  Highcliffe Beach c.1930                           129

# Chapter One

# THE BEGINNINGS

*"Stranger, what e'er thy colour, creed or race*
*Here rest awhile there's virtue in the place."*

During the Second World War wounded servicemen came to Bournemouth to recuperate. Many were invited by Mrs Stuart Wortley to visit Highcliffe Castle. They found there in the quiet beauty of the place an uplifting of the spirit as well as healing of the body. Following an enquiry by medical authorities after the war, it was found that this part of the coast possessed very special healing qualities which helped the wounded to return to health remarkably quickly. This fact was related by Lady Violet Stuart Wortley in her book *Grow old along with me*.

The area to be explored in this book is bounded in the north by the railway line which was built at the end of the 19th century. The eastern boundary is the Walkford Brook which flows through the wooded ravine of Chewton Bunny – a local name for a glen. The western boundary starts at the railway bridge and the Lyndhurst Road (A35) to the Somerford Roundabout, along the Highcliffe Road, turning right into Bure Lane and to the sea.

The ancient history of Highcliffe can only be traced through brief references in documents and records. In the Norman Domesday survey there was a note of a dwelling at Hoburne owned by 'Saulf's wife' – an amazing statement when a woman was regarded at that time as a man's chattel. Later, in 1195, the area now known as Walkford was given to William de Walcford, a guard at Christchurch Castle. There appears to be no record of early dwellings there however, although in the 1880's children from Walkford attended the village school. There are brief references to indicate that, during the reign of Charles I, there was a sea fishery at Chewton which used a special net called a 'ram's horn'.

In the 18th century there were three group of cottages or hamlets at Chewton, Chewton Common and Slop Pond.

Perhaps the earliest of these hamlets was that still standing in Chewton Common Road which was built on part of the Meyrick Estate and, until twenty five to thirty years ago, still had the Forest rights of grazing. These cottages are protected by the Town and Country Planning Act of 1971 and are Grade II listed buildings which indicates that they are cottages of special historical interest. Although the interiors of the cottages have been modernized the original appearance of the exterior has been carefully maintained.

The date 1666 is carved into one of the beams in Number 35 which was once a coach house with living accommodation above for the groom. Number 37 was reputedly a school for waifs and strays called 'Little Meg's School'. Number 33, it is believed, was a forge and Gorse Cottage in 1760 was known to be a 'Meeting Place' or a chapel.

'LITTLE MEGS'

The first semblance of a village in the centre of the area rejoiced in the name of Slop Pond. This was a group of mud walled and thatched roof cottages built at the side of the track from Christchurch to Lymington. They stood approximately to the west of Sea Corner with the pond near the present Sports and Social Club. For what reason were those cottages built in that particular place? Were they an insalubrious group intent on defying the law and engaging in smuggling activities? Or were they fisher folk? Or did they take part in a range of nefarious activities? There was an occasion in Chewton Bunny toward the end of the 19th century when a notorious poacher, Clarke by name, was caught in the act by the son of one of the landowners and the poacher threatened to 'beat his brains out'. When he was arrested later his friends at Slop Pond made effigies of the landowner and his gamekeepers and burnt them publicly on a bonfire in the village.

SEA CORNER

About 1830 Captain Hopkins of Hoburne bought a field at Slop Pond on which he built about twenty houses which extended from Stanley Road westwards. The inhabitants objected to the name Slop Pond and the name of the village was changed, unimaginatively, to Newtown. In 1892 a petition was organised by the residents to change the name once more as so many letters were going astray. The Post Office agreed that the name of the village should be changed and so from the beginning of the 20th century Highcliffe could be considered as referring to all the ecclesiastical parish and the civil parish, i.e. including Chewton, Hoburne and Walkford.

The third hamlet at that time, Chewton, was situated near the water-splash where the Walkford Brook crossed the Christchurch and Lymington lane. The cottages housed mainly farm labourers but was once used as a workhouse for making fusee chains. Robert Harvey Cox owned a workshop in Christchurch making fusee chains and had work sent out to New Milton and Chewton. Fusee chains were used in early clocks and watches when the mainspring first replaced the weights as the motive power. This industry was brought to Christchurch by the Huguenot refugees after the revocation of the Edict of Nantes.

Towards the end of the second half of the 18th century smuggling became a major occupation along the South Coast. Agricultural wages were far below subsistence level, so that the local farm labourers provided a ready work force for unloading the heavily laden luggers that had arrived from the continent. The gently sloping, deserted shores of Christchurch Bay were ideal for those engaged in that illegal trade. Chewton Bunny provided the added safety of the deep ravine running right down to the water's edge giving splendid cover to those awaiting the arrival of the boats. Brandy, wines, lace, silk, tea and tobacco were shipped across the Channel by fast luggers, unloaded by local men and taken to safe hiding places in the Forest before the arrival of the Revenue Officers from Christchurch.

A letter from the Custom House in London dated May 30th 1786 gives details of one such landing by John Streeter from the *Civil Usage* lugger: -

100 small flasks of spirit marked 'F
8 tons tea
2,000-3,000 casks of spirits

But to the ordinary law-abiding residents or visitors Chewton Bunny had something else to offer. The Walkford Brook meanders its way past the picturesque Chewton Mill, to the sea, through a thickly wooded ravine which provided a delightful path through which to stroll. The greatest thrill perhaps was to climb the cliffs from the Bunny to see the incomparable view across the silvery sea to the distant Isle of Wight. The whole panoramic view of the coastline from Hurst Castle to Hengistbury Head was spread before the eyes of someone standing on the cliff top near the village of Slop Pond. It was to these cliffs that John Stuart, 3rd Earl of Bute, came.

HIGH CLIFF

4

# Chapter Two

# HIGH CLIFF

John Stuart, 3rd Earl of Bute, was a close friend of Augusta, Princess of Wales. Due to the premature death of her husband, the Prince of Wales, their son, George William Frederick, the future king, regarded Bute as a father figure. It was a natural progression of this relationship that when he came to the throne George III chose Bute as his Prime Minister. He was not a popular choice. He lacked the political experience and he was a Scotsman and therefore regarded, at the time, as a foreigner and a barbarian. He was constantly harassed as he travelled round London in his sedan chair with cries of "Jack Boot must go!" A Club was formed by the most malicious of his enemies who drank to his damnation from glasses shaped like boots.

Lord Bute married Mary Wortley Montagu. They lived the life of fear with their children at Bute House in South Audley Street, London. The family home was frequently besieged and windows were broken. It was said that an underground passage existed to enable the family to escape into the park if the mob became too violent.

During the eleven months he was Prime Minister, Lord Bute negotiated a peace with France. This angered those who were making a profit from the wars. A tax on cider, which he introduced, was unpopular with the poor. He had tried to be an honest politician but had failed. He resigned and left London, a melancholy and disillusioned man.

He was a wealthy man with houses at Luton and Kenwood and at Lansdown House in London, but his main interests were in the arts and sciences. He financed the setting up of Kew Gardens and endowed the Pagoda. It was to these interests that he now turned. He immersed himself in the study of plants. It was while he was searching for botanical specimens in the New Forest that he came to the high cliffs surrounding Christchurch Bay. He was so thrilled with the view that he camped on the cliffs and subsequently engaged the architect, Robert Adam, to build him a house there.

The house was called High Cliff and was completed by 1773. It was typically Georgian and very similar to others Adam had built for Lord Bute. It contained thirty bedrooms, two libraries, a morning room, drawing room, dining room, breakfast room, study, a 41-foot salon, an organ room, a laboratory, natural history and fossil room, a 250-foot conservatory, a riding house and stables for ten horses. In the organ room there was an unusual organ which was worked by water and played popular tunes.

LOUISA, MARCHIONESS OF WATERFORD

A letter dated 1788 from Lord Bute's daughter, Louisa, to her sister tells her of the house: -

"This house has increased more than four-fold since I saw it but it is the most comfortable that ever I was in. All the rooms face to the sea front and there seems to be no end to them. You come first to the dining room which has a door into the garden, then there is a small ante room, then a room with a bow window leading into another 40-feet long. My father has his laboratory and two libraries and many more cupboards and closets than I ever saw in an old house. My bedchamber and dressing room are over their bedchamber, the prettiest rooms you ever saw, all plainly furnished compared to Luton, but perfect, neat and pretty, my sitting room is painted like Charles' thatched house at Bure, and by the same man, so pretty I wish I could carry it wherever I go."

(from *Magic in the Distance* by V.S. Wortley)

Lord Bute collected books and possessed a valuable and interesting library together with many works of art. But it was the gardens which were his main interest. They were enclosed by walls and greenhouses containing many unusual specimens. There were foreign trees, some of which can still be seen today in the gardens. A camphor tree grew and flowered there. In the grounds too were erected four temples or summerhouses, two were open and two closed. In 1790 Lord Bute was walking along the cliffs when he slipped and fell. One report said he was chastising a small dog and another that he was reaching for a rare flower. He sustained severe injuries but lived for a further two years in great pain. He died in 1792.

Lord Bute's son, Lord Mountstuart, informed the King of his death and received the following reply: -

Queen's House
March 1792

"It is with heartfelt concern I received Lord Mountstuart's account of the death of his late father..."

Lord Mountstuart, now the 4th Earl of Bute, when looking through the late Earl's papers, was deeply moved to find many letters from the King always addressing him as "My dearest friend..." It seems that George III had written daily to Lord Bute reporting to him the many incidents that occurred both at Court and in Parliament and these letters were couched in the most affectionate terms.

It was not long after the death of Lord Bute that High Cliff had to be demolished. The cliff was constantly falling and the space between the House and the edge of the cliff was narrowing until, when only sixty feet remained, the house was pulled down. Only the two Adam lodges on the Lymington Road and, nearer the cliff, part of the riding stables remain to this day. It is still possible to see some of the stones of the old House by paddling out to sea and looking under the water.

The High Cliff Estate remained overgrown and neglected for a number of years.

## TO ONE OF LOVE MOST WORTHY

We saw it enter at the stately portal
And in the lofty Hall take up its stand
A form of marble, pure almost immortal,
Wrought with the genius of a master hand.

From loving hearts to one of love most worthy
Such is the greeting we to thee inscribe;
And never walked on earth the one more worthy
Of homage such as these few words describe.

This tribute of our deep and true affection
Dear Lady! do we now present to thee
In whom we see fair womanhood's perfection,
High thoughts, great aims and meek humility.

Thou walkest onward in thy strength and beauty
The light of goodness beaming from thy face;
Fulfilling all the daily round of duty
With singleness of heart and gentle grace.

Thy presence equal joys and gladness showers
O'er the wild moorlands of thy Border home,
Or on the fairyland of shrubs and flowers,
Fringed by the Channel's restless surging foam.

Who is there unto whom it hath been granted,
To wander in this region for a time,
But has not surely felt himself transplanted
Into a purer and serener clime?

A realm of fancies and of wondrous glory,
Where the free joyous mind at will may rove
Or dream and muse as in some ancient story
Bathed in the sunshine of a world of love.

Where genius lifts her lamp on high, revealing
A mellow richness in life's common things,
Where art and music wake a deeper feeling
And soothe the soul with tender murmurings.

He who hath known all this, once more returning
Into the ruder walks of life again,
Will feel a nobler zeal within him burning
A kinder impulse to his fellow men.

Then Lady! Marvel not that we have striven
Part of our debt of gratitude to pay
Since thou from thy sweet life to us hast given
Bright thoughts and hopes which cannot pass away.

*To Louisa, Marchioness of Waterford, on the coming home of her statue*

August 1st 1876

STATUE OF
LOUISA,
MARCHIONESS OF
WATERFORD

9

# OWNERS OF HIGHCLIFFE CASTLE

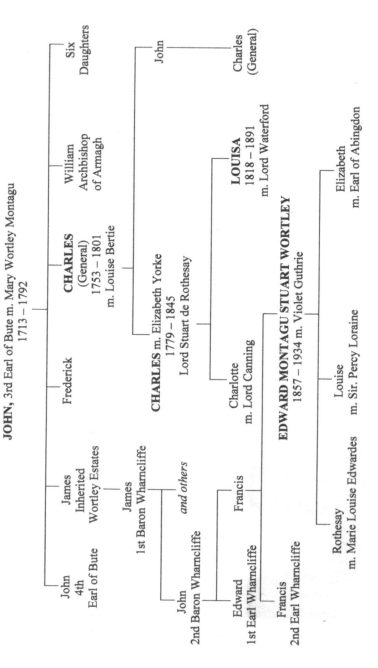

JOHN, 3rd Earl of Bute m. Mary Wortley Montagu
1713 – 1792

James Inherited Wortley Estates — Frederick — CHARLES (General) 1753 – 1801 m. Louise Bertie — William Archbishop of Armagh — Six Daughters

John 4th Earl of Bute

James 1st Baron Wharncliffe

John 2nd Baron Wharncliffe — *and others*

Edward 1st Earl Wharncliffe — Francis

Francis 2nd Earl Wharncliffe

Rothesay m. Marie Louise Edwardes

CHARLES m. Elizabeth Yorke 1779 – 1845 Lord Stuart de Rothesay — John

Charlotte m. Lord Canning — LOUISA 1818 – 1891 m. Lord Waterford — Charles (General)

EDWARD MONTAGU STUART WORTLEY 1857 – 1934 m. Violet Guthrie

Louise m. Sir. Percy Loraine — Elizabeth m. Earl of Abingdon

# Chapter Three

## OWNERS OF THE HIGHCLIFFE ESTATE

### Lord Bute 1713-1792

John Stuart, 3rd Earl of Bute, Viscount Kingarth, Lord Mountstuart, Cumra and Inchmarnoch and Hereditary Keeper of the Castle of Bute was descended from John Stuart, a son of King Robert II of Scotland (1371-1390).

When Lord Bute died he left the High Cliff estate to his fourth and favourite son, Charles Stuart.

### Sir Charles Stuart 1753-1801

Charles Stuart entered the army at the age of fifteen and steadily rose in the ranks. When he inherited High Cliff he was a colonel. He had no desire to live as a country gentleman as his whole life was centred round the army. Shortly after inheriting High Cliff he became a Major General and was given an important command in the Mediterranean where he captured Corsica from the French in 1794 and Minorca from the Spanish in 1798.

BURE HOMAGE

For this victory he was made a Knight Commander of the Order of the Bath. He was not interested in High Cliff and could not afford to maintain it. He decided to sell most of the estate but retained Bure Cottage (Bure Homage) and some farm property at the western end of the estate. There he installed his wife Louisa (née Louisa Bertie, daughter and co-heir of Lord Vere Bertie) and their two sons, Charles and John. He became M.P. for Poole from 1796-1801. General Sir Charles Stuart died at the Thatched House, Richmond, where he was a Ranger of Richmond Park. There is a wall memorial in St Andrews Chapel, Westminster Abbey, to his memory. The tablet was designed by Nollekens and below the name of General Charles Stuart, K.C.B. is that of his son, John.

The main part of the estate was bought by Mr Penleaze.

**Mr. James Penleaze 1754-1819**

Very little is known about this man. He inherited a moderate sum of money and a house. Whilst turning out the house Mr Penleaze came across a cocked-hat box containing no hat but stuffed full of banks notes amounting to a very large sum. With this money he purchased part of the High Cliff estate and in 1794 built himself a very modest house only two hundred yards from the site of the old High Cliff House.

**Lord Stuart de Rothesay 1779-1845**

Charles Stuart grew up at Bure Homage with his brother John. He joined the diplomatic corps and was posted to Vienna and later St. Petersberg. He then became the special envoy of the British Government to Spain and later became British Minister at Lisbon. In recognition of this work he was created Knight Commander of the Order of the Bath. His next assignment was as British Minister to Paris followed by a term at The Hague. When the Duke of Wellington resigned as British Ambassador to the French Court, Sir Charles Stuart took his place.

On February 6th 1816 he married Lady Elizabeth Yorke, third daughter of the 3rd Earl of Hardwicke. They had two daughters, Charlotte Elizabeth (1817) and Louisa Anne (1818).

Further terms of diplomatic service followed in Portugal and Brazil and in recognition of that work Sir Charles became Lord Stuart de Rothesay. He was offered the job of Foreign Minister in the Duke of Wellington's Government but declined as he expressed a preference to return as Ambassador to Paris. As a young boy Charles had vowed that one day he would buy back the High Cliff estate. This he did and built the present Highcliffe Castle. In 1844 Lord Stuart became ill with a nervous paralysis which deprived him of the use of his legs. The last year of his life was spent at Highcliffe where he died in November 1845. He was buried in the crypt of St. Mark's Church, Highcliffe, which he himself had built in 1843. His eldest daughter, Charlotte, married Lord Canning and died of a fever in 1861 in

12

India. His second daughter, Louisa, married the Marquis of Waterford and it was she who inherited Highcliffe Castle on the death of her mother on June 23rd 1867. Lady Stuart was buried at her husband's side in the crypt of St. Mark's.

## Louisa, Lady Waterford  1818-1891

Louisa married the Marquis of Waterford in 1843. He was killed in a hunting accident at Curraghmore in 1859. Lady Waterford spent her widowhood equally between her estate at Ford Castle in Northumberland and Highcliffe Castle. She had a tremendous circle of friends both at Court where she was a friend of Queen Victoria and among the residents of Newtown (as Highcliffe was then known). She visited the poor and the sick of the village and read the Bible to them. She was a gifted artist and musician.

During the time she was in residence at Highcliffe Castle many famous people stayed or visited her. Many of the royal family came over from Osborne House; the Prince of Wales (later becoming King Edward VII) was a frequent visitor. Opera singers, diplomats, architects and foreign royalty all received a warm welcome. She was so loved by all that her friends made a collection and commissioned Sir Edgar Boehme to carve a statue of her in 1870. On the base of the statue were the words: -

*From loving hearts to one of love most worthy*

Lady Waterford left Highcliffe Castle on November 14th 1890 and died at Ford Castle on 12th May 1891. There were no children of her marriage and Highcliffe passed to her second cousin, Major General Edward Stuart Wortley, C.M.G.

## Major General Edward Stuart Wortley  1857-1934

Edward Stuart Wortley went to Eton when he was seven years old. He was closely related to the Earls of Wharncliffe. He married Violet Guthrie at St Peters Church, Eaton Square, London; the officiating clergyman was the Vicar of Highcliffe, Rev. A.D.C. Ryder. Part of their honeymoon was spent at Highcliffe. Edward Stuart Wortley followed a military career with appointments in many European capitals, the Middle East, South Africa and India. He took part in the Battle of Omdurman and in the Boer War and in 1902 became Military Attaché in Paris. Although the Stuart Wortleys travelled extensively they regarded Highcliffe as their home. They entertained frequently and once again many famous people visited the Castle: British and foreign royalty, military and naval personalities, politicians, people famous in all walks of life. In 1907 His Imperial Majesty, German Emperor Wilhelm II – the Kaiser – made his historic visit to Highcliffe Castle.

There were three children of the marriage, Rothesay, who became a fighter pilot and died before his father and mother; Louise, who married Sir Percy Loraine

13

and Elizabeth who married Montagu Bertie, who later inherited the Earldom of Abingdon.

On the death of Major General Edward Stuart Wortley in 1934, Highcliffe was left to Marie Louise Stuart Wortley, the widow of Rothesay Stuart Wortley, who died in 1948.

## Lord Abingdon

Lord Abingdon bought Highcliffe from Mrs Marie Stuart Wortley, thus enabling Mrs. Violet Stuart Wortley, his mother-in-law, to reside at the Castle until it was finally sold outside the family in 1950. Mrs. Violet Stuart Wortley moved to the Mill House, Chewton Glen, prior to her death in 1953.

## Mr. J.H. Lloyd

Mr Lloyd was the proprietor of an acetate works in Christchurch. He planned to use the Castle as a children's convalescent home. He decorated all the rooms and laid thick linoleum on the floors. It was planned to care for 75 children at a cost to their parents of four guineas a week but this venture was not a success.

HIGHCLIFFE CASTLE c.1950
(Rothesay Drive and castle extension as yet un-built)

## The Claretian Major Seminary

The Congregation of the Sons of the Immaculate Heart of Mary (or the Claretian Missionaries) purchased Highcliffe Castle in August 1953, together with

14

10 acres of land. The remainder was sold for development purposes. The Claretians first came to England in 1912 and founded houses at Hayes, Loughton and Bristol. The college at Highcliffe had thirty students training for the priesthood. They wore rough brown cassocks with a white cord round their waists. The college was moved to Oxford in 1965 because it was said that there was not sufficient outside academic stimulus such as libraries and museums in this area for the students. Once again the Castle was for sale.

### Three Local Businessmen

The Castle was bought by three local businessmen. Planning applications for the development of parts of the Castle grounds for residential purposes were submitted but these were rejected.

### Christchurch Borough Council

Christchurch Borough Council bought the Castle and opened the grounds to the public on June 4th 1977 in commemoration of the Silver Jubilee of the accession to the throne of Her Majesty Queen Elizabeth II. Since then parts of the Castle have been renovated and opened to the public.

HIGHCLIFFE CASTLE

15

# Chapter Four

# HIGHCLIFFE CASTLE I

The 'Castle' might be said to have started when the High Cliff estate was bought from Charles Stuart by a Mr. Penleaze who built a rough-cast house with two bow windows to the end rooms about 200 yards from the original High Cliff House. This is still standing and is known as the Penleaze Wing of the present Castle.

It was probably whilst he was still the British Ambassador in Paris that Lord Stuart de Rothesay fulfilled his life's ambition to buy back the family estate of High Cliff, thus satisfying the family motto – *Avito Viret Honore* – He flourishes in an honourable ancestry.

Lord Stuart selected and shipped across the Channel some beautiful ancient stonework from L'Abbaye de Jumièges and from La Grande Maison des Andelys, near Rouen. Working together with his architect, Donthorn, between 1830 and 1835 they built onto the old house of Mr Penleaze.

Lady Stuart spent much of her time visiting her mother, Lady Hardwicke, who was dying, so that Lord Stuart had a completely free hand to indulge his hobby of building. The architect, Donthorn, was anxious to make his name so between them they were adding room after room. What had originally been planned as a small villa was now a building something between a church and a castle. When Lady Stuart returned to Highcliffe and saw the result she was horror-stricken and persuaded Donthorn to reduce the number of rooms by a third but she was unable to make him do away with the pinnacles and ecclesiastical external decorations. In the open work on the parapet facing the sea are the words of Lucretius from his second book *De Rerum Natura*: -

*"Suave, mari magno turbantibus aequora ventis e terra*
*magnum alterius spectare laborem."*

"Sweet it is when on the great sea the winds are buffeting the waters,
To look from the land on another's great struggles."

Above the Great Portico, carved in stone, stood the heraldic stag holding the Stuart banner. One of the more beautiful features of the building was the ornate oriel window which came from the Grande Maison des Andelys and was called the King's Oriel Window. It was said that Anthony, King of Navarre, died in the Manor House in 1562 after the Siege of Rouen, in the room lit by this oriel window. The room at Highcliffe contained the following inscription over the carved mantelpiece: -

*Antoyne de Bourbon, Roy de Navarre mourut 1562 a La Grande Maison des Andelys, Normandie. Dans la chambre du quel Maison la Fenestre de cet appartement fut transporté ici.*

HIGHCLIFFE CASTLE ORIEL WINDOW

Lady Stuart, in her letters did not appear to have any great regard for Donthorn's capabilities. She was annoyed he spent so much of his time with the exterior decorations and so little with the real essentials of building a home. She objected to the "ill contrived bits of bedrooms of all shapes and sizes – and to be squeezed up in such wretched bedrooms stamps him as totally unfit to plan a house". So despondent was she that she wrote: -

"I wish the whole thing had fallen over the cliff and I hope I shall not throw myself over it in utter despair."

Whilst the building was being carried out the family moved from Bure Homage to live in the Penleaze wing. From Bure they moved the old French tapestries and furniture which Lord Stuart had purchased whilst in Paris from the hotel of Marshal Ney all marked with a large 'N' and the Marshal's baton and chairs which had belonged to Napoleon I having a carved ornament in the arms for snuff. Lord Stuart soon accepted Highcliffe Castle and set to work laying out the gardens. The two lodges, the kitchen garden and the riding stables were all that remained of the old house. On the actual site stood a sundial, a rough stone block ornamented with cables and dolphins and supported by a kneeling angel. Lady Stuart planted many evergreen oaks, which she called "nine pennies" because that is what they cost at the time.

A way down to the beach was made to Lord Bute's Gap where there were bathing machines. Later Lord Stuart brought an old steamer round from Southampton and beached her there to be used as a sea-lodge. This was converted into a dwelling of two rooms and a kitchen and was looked after by three interesting characters, a man called Whitcher with a miserable wife, and a golden-haired little girl. The path to the beach was levelled to enable a pony trap to be driven down. The steamer was not a satisfactory dwelling as it became damp and smelled and Bemister, a carpenter, was commissioned to build a small cottage there.

During the years that followed the Castle became the home of many treasures including those which had been accumulated during the Stuarts' assignments abroad and many gifts from visiting celebrities.

The stained glass windows were most interesting. In the Great Hall at the northern end was a magnificent window. It was said that the central part of the glass was taken from the church of St. Vigor in Rouen and dated about 1547. The remainder of the window was made of pieces from the Adoration of the Magi dated 1425 and the Last Judgement, probably 15th century German. Lady Waterford recounts in her recollections: -

"A complete old window had been brought for the hall; but the framework of Donthorn's window at the end was four times bigger. We fitted it by extending the pattern on all sides and pressing into service such mutilated bits of glass as we could turn into other figures, adding a glory round the head of one saint, a mantle to another and palms and wings from Holloway [a glazier in Christchurch]. The window to this day would scarcely be supposed to be so enormously stretched from its original dimensions."

(*Two Noble Lives* by Augustus Hare)

In the centre library was a large Gothic bay window containing 17th century Flemish glass. In the Winter Garden were two stained glass windows presented by the Kaiser to commemorate his visit in 1907. Above the fireplace was a large window divided by undecorated mullions into six equal lights depicting various saints and the Rothesay Shield. In the drawing room was a beautiful window showing the coats of arms of the Stuarts, Yorkes and Berties.

GREAT HALL SHOWING JESSE WINDOW

As well as the statue of Lady Waterford in the Winter Garden stood a small statue of a child with the word 'Bettine' at the base. It was of Elizabeth Stuart Wortley in the fancy dress of Joan of Arc for a party. Her father, General Stuart Wortley, was so taken with her appearance he commissioned the statue to be made.

The main rooms on the ground floor were the Great Portico, the Great Hall and the Garden Porch, the Octagonal Hall, the Dining Room, the Drawing Room, the Ante Library and Library and the Winter Garden.

The Great Portico was the main entrance to the Castle. It was here that the carriages of the nobility drew up and the passengers alighted. The French historian, Deshayes, records that this beautiful archway was the entrance to the great cellar at Jumièges. The archway was broken up and re-assembled together with some contemporary stonework. To make the stonework appear as one, the whole was distempered to make a uniform colour. It is possible to distinguish today which is the older stonework as it is more porous and has absorbed and retained the distemper whilst the contemporary stonework has lost its colouring.

LA GRANDE MAISON DES ANDELYS

The Great Portico led into the Great Hall. Reginald Pound, in his book *Selfridge*, maintains that this room had been a chapel standing in the grounds of a French chateau. The first impression was one of great height. The hammer-beam roof stood 60 feet above the ground. There was a beautiful inverted U-shaped staircase leading to the upper rooms which ran up each side of the Hall with a balcony in the centre where the two flights of stairs met.

From the garden porch, where Lady Waterford used to make tea, a door led to the Octagonal Hall which was traditionally the Music Room and was decorated with Louis XV boiseries. Lord Stuart had bought these whilst in Paris. The Drawing Room was decorated in full Louis XV style and on the walls hung the Gobelin tapestries which came from the Palace of the Knights of St John in Valetta. Lady Waterford sold these in 1889 for £3,000 to pay for cliff stabilization and drainage works. She engaged the services of an engineer who built an elaborate drainage system in the cliffs below the Castle, the success of which is still visible today.

THE DINING ROOM

The Dining Room possessed a fine marble fireplace. Both the Ante Library and the Library were galleried and capable of housing 30,000 books. The Library had an interesting cupboard cleverly concealed as bookshelves. This cupboard was planned to house the machinery for an organ which was to have been installed in the Octagonal Room. The doors leading to the Winter Garden were similarly disguised as bookshelves. The Castle was hidden from view on the landward side and it was only possible to see it by boarding a steamer at Bournemouth pier and sailing past the site.

THE DRAWING ROOM

The Castle was then bought by the Roman Catholic Order of Claretian Missionaries to use as a seminary. The Claretians made one or two innovations to the building. They laid the gravel drive from Rothesay Drive to the Castle and they built a rather ugly extension to the southern side of the Castle adjoining the Penleaze Wing which is now used as a café. They converted the Great Hall into a chapel by removing the beautiful staircase and building a high altar. Around the altar was the shrine of the Immaculate Heart of the Blessed Virgin Mary. Both the Claretian students and villagers worshipped here.

Before the sale of the Castle by the Claretians in 1965 and again in 1967, the Castle was badly damaged by fire. When Christchurch Borough Council took over the property the Castle itself was considered too unsafe to allow the public near. Through the high wire fence which surrounded the building it was possible to see some of the exterior grandeur of Highcliffe Castle but the interior was in ruins.

HIGHCLIFFE CASTLE – THE GREAT HALL
By permission of Rowland Adams, A.I.P.

23

HIGHCLIFFE CASTLE – THE CHAPEL
By permission of Rowland Adams, A.I.P.

# HIGHCLIFFE CASTLE HAMPSHIRE
## Ground Plan

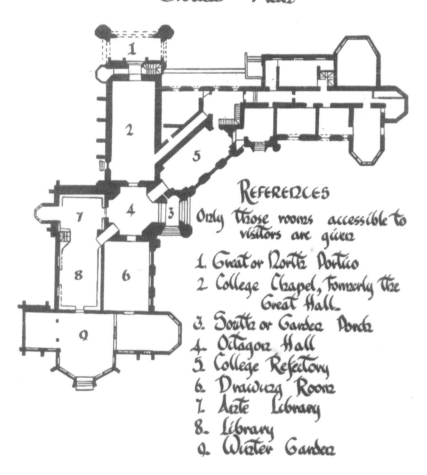

REFERENCES

Only those rooms accessible to
visitors are given

1. Great or North Portico
2. College Chapel, formerly the
    Great Hall.
3. South or Garden Porch
4. Octagon Hall
5. College Refectory
6. Drawing Room
7. Ante Library
8. Library
9. Winter Garden

# VISITORS TO THE CASTLE

The Castle was the centre of the social life for the gentry for miles around. Dinner parties, lunches, afternoon tea, musical evenings and dances were eagerly anticipated. Besides local friends the Castle had many visitors from London society from Court and from abroad. It would be impossible to compose a complete list of all who have visited the Castle. When the family were not in residence the Castle was rented by many wealthy people among whom were: -

**Sir John Aird**, who was the engineering contractor and had been responsible for the construction of the Crystal Palace and the damming of the River Nile at Assam. He was M.P. for North Paddington and stayed at the Castle from 1891.

**George Nathaniel**, Marquess of Curzon, leased the Castle whilst he was Viceroy of India because his wife was too unwell to travel to India with him.

**Sir Alfred Cooper**, a surgeon, hired the Castle in 1907 and was actually in residence when the Castle was requested for the Kaiser to use.

**Mr Gordon Selfridge**, the famous American-born founder of the Oxford Street store of Selfridge & Co. of London, rented the Castle on several occasions and developed a particular affection for the area. He contemplated building himself a palace on Hengistbury Head. In 1929 he bought the Head but sold it to Bournemouth Corporation in 1930. He is buried in St. Mark's churchyard where his wife, Lois, and his mother Rose, are also interred.

But perhaps the most memorable visits were those made to the family in residence:-
... in 1889 by Mr. and Mrs. Gladstone;
... in 1892 by the Duke and Duchess of Connaught
(Prince Arthur, 3rd son of Queen Victoria);
... in 1907 by the Kaiser.

### Mr and Mrs Gladstone at Highcliffe – July 1889

A newspaper article of the time records the visit of Mr and Mrs Gladstone: -
"The inhabitants of this picturesque neighbourhood were in a state of excitement on Sunday owing to the unexpected visit of Mr. and Mrs. Gladstone, who were the guests of the most hon. Louisa, Marchioness of Waterford at Highcliffe Castle from Saturday to Monday. The intended visit was kept a profound secret, except to two or three persons. But the report spread when a telegram was received at Hinton Admiral Station to say that the down express, due at Bournemouth at 7.48 would stop at Hinton to allow Mr. and Mrs. Gladstone to alight, and that the 11.10 up express from

Bournemouth, would also stop on Monday to take them up to town again ... the right hon. gentleman and his wife arrived at Highcliffe Castle about 8 p.m. on Saturday. They were met at the front entrance by the Marchioness of Waterford who gave them a warm greeting and a cordial welcome ... We believe we are correct in stating that Mr. Gladstone has never visited Highcliffe before, although he has been expected on several occasions but he has previously visited Lady Waterford at Ford Castle, her residence in the north ... The quiet and picturesque surroundings, as also the bright service at the little parish church, not failing to make an indelibly favourable impression upon both of their minds ... hence it was not surprising that the railway station was apparently quiet when the train pulled up. A fortunate few, however, including a cricketing team from Bournemouth happened to be on the platform awaiting the arrival of the ordinary 8.06 train ...They raised a very enthusiastic cheer, to which the ex-Premier and his wife bowed their acknowledgements. The distinguished visitors entered the carriage and pair waiting for them, and reached Highcliffe in a few minutes ... and when Mr. and Mrs. Gladstone appeared at church on Sunday morning there was a large congregation assembled ... distinguished visitors occupied seats in Lady Waterford's pew and were accompanied by her ladyship and other visitors. It was hoped by many persons that Mr. Gladstone would have read the lessons, but he was obliged to decline on account of the state of his voice. After the service the party returned to Highcliffe walking leisurely, and most of the congregation assembled in the avenue to see them pass and the right hon. gentleman frequently returned greetings which were accorded him by raising his hat. We understand that the party at luncheon included, besides the Marchioness of Waterford and Mr. & Mrs. Gladstone, Lady Jane and Mr. Ellice, The Rev. John Ellis and Mr. Bellairs. Mr. and Mrs. Gladstone rested quietly indoors during the afternoon, the rooms occupied by them while at the Castle being those known as the Green rooms. This suite of rooms are situated on the ground floor and from them a splendid view across the grounds and out to sea is to be obtained."

**The Royal Visit to Highcliffe and Christchurch**

In the Parish Magazine the visit of the Duke and Duchess of Connaught was reported: -

"Their Royal Highnesses The Duke and Duchess of Connaught have paid a brief visit to Major and Mrs. Stuart Wortley at Highcliffe Castle, arriving on Saturday, October 29th and remaining until the Monday following. On Saturday the Duke and Duchess, with their retinue, travelled in special vehicles attached to the 2.15 p.m. train from Portsmouth and on arrival at Eastleigh just after 3.00 p.m. these vehicles were detached and composed as a special train, ran direct to Hinton Admiral where the train drew up at about 4.00 p.m. The Duke and Duchess travelled in an elegantly furnished royal double saloon. On alighting their Royal Highnesses were greeted by Major Stuart-Wortley and the welcome was most cordial. Both the Royal Visitors extending a warm shake of the hand to their host. The Major conducted his Royal guests to the carriage which was waiting for them. He himself driving his favourite pony cart. The arrival platform was covered in red baize and satisfactory arrangements were made by Mr. Bunny, Station Master, for the convenience of the party on their arrival. A small crowd of spectators had assembled in the station yard to witness the arrival of the distinguished visitors and P.C. Hawkins of the local police was on duty. The afternoon was beautifully fine, the heavy rains and storms of the two days previous having been succeeded by genial October weather.

Captain Burn accompanied the Duke as Aide-de-Camp and Miss Burn was Lady in Waiting to the Duchess. The house party at Highcliffe during the Royal visit included The Honourable Mrs. Neville Littleton, Captain The Honourable Cecil Bingham, Colonel Lane, Colonel Donald Brown, The Honourable D. Lawless, Mr. Richard Stuart-Wortley, Miss L. Guthrie and Miss Smythe. The Rev. and Mrs. Algernon Ryder were entertained among the guests at luncheon on Sunday and on Monday the luncheon party included the Earl and Countess of Malmesbury, Mr. Albert Nugent and Miss Nugent. On Sunday morning the Royal visitors with the house party attended services at the village church and on Monday drove into Christchurch. Their Royal Highnesses promenaded in the Highcliffe grounds on each day during their visit and on Sunday afternoon they walked through the village of Newtown in which the people whom they met loyally recognised them and the Duke and Duchess graciously acknowledged these signs of loyalty.

The suite of rooms occupied by the illustrious visitors at the Castle were those on the ground floor, known as the Green rooms, possessing a fine sea view. The rooms were all splendidly furnished, much of the furniture being of considerable historic interest, the chairs were once the property of Napoleon I, the excellent silken bed furniture was the work of Marie Antoinette, and the carpet and bed formerly belonged to Marshall Ney, whilst some of the very beautiful Japanese silk adorned the walls. The rooms were the same suite as were occupied by Mr. and Mrs. Gladstone and many of the distinguished people who visited the late Lady Waterford, during her residence at Highcliffe.

As the distinguished party were leaving the house on Monday, in the front hall, the Duke was presented by Miss Ryder, daughter of the Vicar, with a lovely flower which he wore away in his buttonhole and the Duchess was presented with a handsome floral bouquet by Ethel Skinner, daughter of the Highcliffe gardener. The special saloon train which was to convey the Royal party direct to Portsmouth steamed up from Bournemouth arriving at Hinton Admiral soon after half past three. The Duke and Duchess, both of whom looked remarkably well and cheerful, were warmly greeted by the spectators which had assembled on the station platform to witness the departure of the distinguished guests. For several minutes the Duke and Duchess engaged in affable conversation with the Highcliffe party, which had accompanied them to the Station and at 3.45 p.m. the special train steamed away. As the Royal Visitors entered the saloon, at Hinton, three cheers were given by the spectators for the Duke and Duchess."

**The Kaiser at Highcliffe**

In 1907 the German Emperor spent three weeks at Highcliffe Castle. He was the son of Princess Victoria and Frederick (Emperor of Germany) and the grandson of Queen Victoria.

Preparing for the visit with only a week's notice was a mammoth task for the Colonel and Mrs Stuart Wortley. There was not sufficient room at the Castle for all the Emperor's suite so accommodation had to be found in the village for them. It was discovered that the Germans preferred a Sitz-bad (bidet) to the conventional bathroom. Colonel Stuart Wortley went into Bournemouth, purchased a lorry load of Sitz-bad and had them fitted in readiness for his guests. Two underground rooms were set apart as a Post Office to deal with the multitude of state business. A telegraph machine and two telephones were installed.

Catering was left in the capable hands of Mrs. Rosa Lewis. The first meal was nearly a disaster. Quails were on the menu but the knife-and-fork tool the Kaiser used with his good hand (the Kaiser had a withered arm) could not cope with the slippery bird.

A newspaper report on the catering arrangements for the Kaiser and his suite states that it was a gargantuan affair. As far as possible everything had been bought in the village but the demands of the 120 inhabitants of the Castle was more than the village could supply and wagon loads of provisions were brought down from London. During the three weeks there had been consumed: -

10,060lbs. beef and mutton
42 sides bacon
1,050 chickens
5,000 eggs
2,100lbs. apples
1,870lbs. pears
300 game pies
2,000 loaves bread
84 hams

A pattern for the visit soon emerged. The morning started for H.I.M. with a cold bath of seawater which was brought up from the beach in two buckets by one of the groundsmen. These had to be delivered to the Kaiser's room by 8 a.m. After breakfast the Emperor dealt with state matters. In the afternoon a fleet of cars would arrive to conduct the Kaiser and his suite on a sightseeing tour of the neighbourhood. He visited some of the homes of the local gentry, Crichel, Newlands, Somerley, Beaulieu, Romsey and, of course, Christchurch Priory. He admired the tone of the organ in the Priory but commented that the casing was rather shabby. He later offered to replace the old casing with a new one. In memory of his visit to Highcliffe Castle the Kaiser planted an oak tree in the Pasture (now part of Rothesay Drive).

It was a well-known fact that the Kaiser loved children. Before he left Highcliffe he gave a tea party for the children of the village. Everyone in the village lent candlesticks for the occasion and the tables were laid with cakes, apples and oranges and with nuts, sweets and crackers. Towering above it all was the most amazing cake made by the cook at the Castle on the Kaiser's instructions. It stood six feet high, a mountain of sugar confection, which the Kaiser had to stab three times before he could cut the first slice. Newspaper reports of the time said that the Kaiser had never looked happier – "he was bubbling over with merriment".

When the Emperor's visit to Highcliffe came to an end he invited Colonel Stuart-Wortley to Germany to watch the manoeuvres of the German Grand Army the following year. Mrs Stuart-Wortley received the following telegram: -

"Sincerest thanks for lovely photograph and kind letter. Wish once more to express my deepest gratitude to you for allowing me to stay at your lovely place with which I am quite in love. I am so glad that His Majesty (Edward VII) has agreed to my inviting your husband to our manoeuvres next year. With warmest wishes for a Happy New Year to you and your children and the Colonel."

**Below is a record of some of the Castle's distinguished visitors**

1859    Queen Marie Amelia, wife of King Louis Phillipe of France (1830-48), called to visit her old friend, Lady Stuart de Rothesay in September.

1872    Queen Sophie Matilda (1818-77), wife of King William III of Netherlands.
        Adelaide Kemble and her husband, Charles Edward Sartoris, visited the Castle in July. Miss Kemble sang at Covent Garden Opera House.

1874    Lady Caroline Charteris (1816-91), youngest daughter of Earl of Charteris, was described by Augustus Hare as "of plain exterior but in mind indescribably beautiful."
        Frequent visitors to the Castle at this time were Lady Jane Ellice and

Mr. William Ellice, personal friends of Lady Waterford, who used to spend the summer months at Highcliffe. Canon Augustus Hare was another frequent visitor and wrote the life of Lady Waterford and her sister, Lady Canning, in three volumes entitled *The Story of Two Noble Lives.*

1876     Lady Herbert of Lea.
         Lady Constance Leslie and Sir John Leslie.

1879     Crown Prince of Sweden visited in July.
         Marianne Margaret, Viscountess Alford (1816-88) who was the founder of the Royal School of Needlework.

1880     Prince and Princess of Wales landed from the Royal Yacht *Osborne* on August 2nd with their children:

            Prince George (George V)     Princess Victoria
            Princess Louise            Princess Maud
            Princess Royal

         They stayed to tea and the Princes bathed.
         Charles William de la Poer Beresford (1846-1919) came with the Prince of Wales.

1881     Crown Princess of Germany, Princess Victoria and Crown Prince Frederick with their children Victoria, Sophia and Margarete.
         Prince of Wales (Edward VII).

1885     Francis, Viscount Knollys (1837-1924) accompanied the Royal party. He was private secretary to the Prince of Wales.
         Prince of Wales.

1889     Mr. and Mrs. Gladstone - their visit was kept secret but the secret was discovered when the train stopped at Hinton Admiral.

1892     The Duke and Duchess of Connaught.

1901     Prince of Wales.

1906     King Alfonso of Spain, Princess Beatrice, Prince Leopold, Prince Maurice of Batternburg. King Alfonso planted a Spanish chestnut in the grounds of the Castle. It flourished but for no accountable reason faded and died a few months before the King abdicated.

1907     Count Paul, A.M.H., Wolff Metternich-zur-Cracht, German Ambassador to England (1901-12); he made arrangements for the Kaiser's visit.
         His Imperial Majesty – The Kaiser – German Emperor Wilhelm II.
         Prince von Bülow (1849-1924), a member of the suite accompanying

the Kaiser. He was German Chancellor.

1914    Sir William Goschen (1847-1924) rented Beacon Lodge and was a
frequent visitor to the Castle.
Sir Edward Lutyens (1869-1944), the architect, was an old friend of
Mrs. Stuart Wortley since childhood days. He designed the Cenotaph.

1926    Dame Nellie Melba (1859-1931) stayed whilst fulfilling a musical
engagement in Bournemouth. She sang Gounod's *Ave Maria* from the
organ loft of St. Mark's Church during the Sunday evening service.
Lord and Lady Forster; he was the Governor-General of Australia,
1920-25. Lady Forster was the daughter of the 1st Baron Montagu.
Beverly Nicholls – journalist and playwright.

1928    Duke of Aosta and his wife, Princess Anne de France, during his stay
at the Castle was invited to Buckingham Palace. He had no suitable
clothes for the occasion and so rang Almonds Hotel in London
requesting them to beg, steal or borrow some suitable clothes for him.
Queen Mary visited whilst staying with Lord Shaftesbury at Wimborne
St. Giles.

QUEEN MARY AT HIGHCLIFFE CASTLE

# Chapter Five

# COUNTRY HOUSES

The Victorian era was the age of the large estates: some had been inherited and others gained through advantageous marriages, while others had been bought with the money made from the thriving industries in the new towns.

In the 19th century Highcliffe comprised many estates, varying in size. Highcliffe Castle predominated. North of the Lymington Road from west to east were the estates of Hoburne, Saulfland, Shelley Hill, Nea House, Cranemoor, Latimers, Holmhurst, Wolhayes and Amberwood. Estate workers lived in the thatched cottages on the estates or at Newtown, Chewton Common or Walkford. South of the Lymington Road, adjoining the Castle, was Cliff Close followed by Beacon Lodge, Culmore and Greystones. Corn was ground at the water mill, Chewton Mill – now the 'Mill House', Chewton Bunny. Gamekeepers used to gather at 'Ye Olde Hoy', an inn, now a private residence called The Hoy.

## HOBURNE

HOBURNE HOUSE

Hoburne means a 'spur by a stream'. The spelling has varied: Hoburna, Hubburne, Hubborn and now Hoburne. This has been a residential site from the time of Edward the Confessor (1005-1066). In the 1830's Captain Hopkins lived at

33

Hoburne. He bought a field in the centre of the present village where he built the houses which were to constitute the new village of Newtown. There have been several houses on the estate, the last one was of Georgian design by Walter Surrel and built between 1912 and 1914.

It is said that an earlier house was used for smuggling activities and that an underground passage existed which enabled smugglers to escape if the approach of the Revenue Officers was reported by the lookouts.

'DOMESDAY OAK'

In the grounds of the house were two Himalayan Pines grown from seeds brought back from India by Lady Canning (Charlotte de Rothesay) whose husband was Viceroy of India. Also within the grounds was the trunk of an oak, the 'Domesday Oak', which according to local folklore is mentioned in the Domesday Survey as marking the southern limit of the New Forest. Although this is subject to dispute, the tree is undoubtedly several hundred years old.

Hoburne was the home for many years of General Charles Stuart of the Grenadier Guards, a cousin of Lady Waterford. After his death in 1892, Admiral Sir Curzon Howe, his nephew, and Lady Curzon Howe lived at Hoburne. Admiral Howe was an aide-de-camp to Queen Victoria and was responsible for the sea training of Prince Albert and Prince George (Later George V). At the close of his sea-going career he flew his flag from the mast of *HMS Victory* as Commander-in-Chief at Portsmouth. When he died he was buried with full naval honours at

34

Highcliffe Parish Church in 1911. The owner in 1912 was Mr. L.G. Browne and later General Gilbert Browne. As a subaltern he served under Lord Baden Powell in South Africa. After his retirement he became the local Commissioner for the Boy Scouts. He took an active part in village life as a churchwarden, in the local Home Guard and in the British Legion.

## SAULFLAND

SAULFLAND

After the death of Admiral Sir Curzon Howe, Lady Howe had Saulflands built, and named the house after the original owner of the land, a Saxon called Saulf. Saulfland suffered incendiary damage during World War II; it may be presumed that the bombs were intended for Christchurch Airfield and not the A.T.S. in occupation in the house at that time. After the war the house was the first converted into flats.

## SHELLEY HILL

A house called Shelley Hill stood north of the Lymington Road opposite the golf course. It was owned at the beginning of the 20th century by Edward Huntly Hooper, a local magistrate.

Built during the 19th century, it was originally called Wood End House, the only record of which is an advertisement for the sale of furniture: -

"April 27th 1889

Short notice of an attractive sale of superior furniture ... fashionable Dog Cart and harness, Park hay etc. Wood End, 2 miles from Christchurch and 7 from Bournemouth ... favoured with instructions from Mrs. Crauford (in consequence of the residence having been let on lease) to sell by auction on Tuesday, May 7th commencing at 11 o'clock, the remaining superior modern furniture and contents of the Mansion comprising Dining and Drawing Room, Morning Room and Library and several Bedchambers."

Its name was changed in 1895 to Shelley Hill.

The author has heard the tale of a clandestine meeting which took place between the daughter of a local gentleman and her lover. The irate gentleman is said to have murdered the lover and the spot was marked by a cross cut into the bark of an oak tree growing from the bank bordering Shelley Hill.

The house was later sold to Miss Harwood who used it as a girls' day and boarding school. It was called St. George's School and was run on Church of England principles. The uniform was Wedgwood blue and girls were accepted from the age of four years to eighteen years and boys from four years to nine years. It remained functional until 1961 and was later demolished to make way for the development of Curzon Way and St. George's Close.

SHELLEY HILL

CRANEMOOR HOUSE

## CRANEMOOR HOUSE

This house was built in the 19th century and has a stucco façade with wide eaves and a recessed square corner tower. The gardens of the house extended to the railway line. The drive left Hinton Wood Avenue a short distance south of the railway station and wound round behind the bungalows in Cranemoor Close. Before the Second World War the house was used as a school for young gentlemen known as Luckham's School. During that war the house was requisitioned to be used by the Fire Service. Cranemoor House is still standing in Cranemoor Avenue and is divided into three separate homes. Part of the old boundary wall and some outbuildings can still be seen at the rear of the houses in Cranemoor Gardens.

## LATIMERS

Latimers was one of the smaller country houses built at the end of the 19th century. Owners have included a Mr. and Mrs. Bains, followed by Rupert Fordham who 'married' Miss Clutterbuck from the Mill House. Mr Fordham owned large estates in the Midlands and took an active interest in local public affairs, being a member both of the local Conservative Association and the Highcliffe Horticultural Association. He died in 1939. Miss Clutterbuck was a well-known local coloratura singer who was responsible for the Gilbert and Sullivan productions in the village during the 1920's. The last owner before the house was demolished was Major Milne. An estate of neo-Georgian houses was built on the site retaining the name of Latimers.

LATIMERS

## NEA HOUSE

The boundaries of the old Nea House estate were Hinton Wood Avenue, Nea Road and Smugglers Lane as far north as the railway line encompassing the estate of Wingfield. The northern part of the estate comprised Nea Wood, a valuable plantation of timber. In 1728 the estate was sold to Charles Brander, father of Gustavus Brander, who spent the last years of his life at Nea House. Nea House was demolished in 1940 and stood opposite Nea Farm House in Nea Road, on the site of the present Nea Meadows. The entrance gate, which can still be seen, is on what was previously called Ice House Hill, so named because an ice-cooled underground game larder had been built at the place. The name of the road is now Hinton Wood Avenue. The house was built of brick and plaster cast with a grey slate roof. The rooms were very large and the Drawing Room measured 28ft x 18ft; the billiard room 32ft x 18ft and there were seven main bedrooms. Outside there was a range of brick and slated buildings with stabling for three horses and garages for two cars. Of particular interest were the engine room and the unique electric light plant which consisted of a .Hornsby 6 h. p. gas engine, dynamo and battery room which housed twenty seven cells. The unit produced and stored electricity at 50 volts which was used to light the house.

The gardens consisted of beautifully kept lawns, a large variety of rhododendrons, a small park with a stream and woodlands. Included in the estate were Spring Cottage, a gardener's cottage, and two bungalows near Hinton Admiral Station. The whole estate covered 169 acres and was sold on July 14th 1938 in seven lots for development. Nea House, however, remained until 1940 and was the home of Commander Roger Twysden, R.N.

Several occupants of Nea House have claim to fame. The Camerons, a family of high-ranking military men, lived there in the 19th and 20th centuries. An early record of the Camerons is that of the death of Lt. Col. William Gordon Cameron in 1856. He had served in the Grenadier Guards and fought in the Peninsular War, being attached to the staff of the great Duke at the crowning victory of the Battle of Waterloo where he lost his right arm.

NEA HOUSE

His funeral was reported in the St. Mark's Parish Magazine, dated June 7th 1856: -

"On Tuesday the mortal remains of the late Lt. Col. W.G. Cameron whose death was recorded in our last issue, were conveyed to the family vault in the church of Highcliffe. The procession was headed by the Mutes and the usual attendants. The funeral service was impressively read by the incumbent, the Rev. Dobson."

Perhaps the best-known Cameron in the village was General Sir William Cameron, C.B, V.D., K.C.B. of the Kings Own Royal Lancashire Regiment. His banner now rests in the South Quire aisle of Christchurch Priory. It was consecrated on July 22nd 1913 in the Henry VIII Chapel in Westminster Abbey where his memorial plate remains. When the estate was sold in 1938 the owner at that time was Major General N.J.G. Cameron, C.B., C.M.G.

Towards the end of the 19th century, Lady Amphlett, daughter of Mr. C.

Martin of neighbouring Belvedere (later Marydale Convent) was one of the residents. Lady Amphlett's name appeared frequently in the Parish Magazines of the 1880's as being the organiser of various charities such as the Clothing Club, the Boot and Shoe Club and the Sunday School.

## HOLMHURST

The Holmhurst estate stretched from Hinton Wood Avenue in the west to Cranemoor Chapel in the east. The northern boundary may be roughly estimated as Pinewood Road and the southern boundary as Braemar Drive. The main entrance was from Hinton Wood Avenue where the small red-bricked Lodge, which was the gardener's home, stood until late last century. The original drive to the house swept to the north of the Lakewood pond through thickets of rhododendrons. The house was built in the early Victorian style and had a separate bell tower which housed a clock. There was a large, imposing iron-studded front door. The entrance hall was dominated by a beautiful wooden staircase. Each rung of the banisters was carved with rabbits and squirrels. The butler's and chauffeur's houses are still standing in Chewton Common Road but Holmhurst itself was demolished about 1960.

HOLMHURST

The earliest known resident of Holmhurst was Sir John Thursby, a very popular character in the village. He was elected a churchwarden of St. Mark's Church and re-elected sometime later in spite of his frequent absences from the district. He gave the church choir annual supper parties which appeared to have been hilarious.

The earliest reference to Holmhurst was the announcement of the wedding of Sir John's daughter: -

"October 13th 1888

A marriage is arranged and will take place between Mr Willoughby Aston Littledale of Bolton Hall and Miss Violet Thursby of Ormerod House, Burnley, Lancs. and Holmhurst, near Christchurch, Hants."

Sir John was a sportsman who enjoyed hunting and shooting. At Holmhurst he kept a pack of harriers of fifteen couples. The horn was carried by his son, George, who was reputedly and excellent rider. The parties and dances were eagerly anticipated by all the young gentry. Newspaper records report that the festivities often continued until 3 o'clock in the morning and that the tables were laid with gold plate.

The last residents were Mr. and Mrs. Pike. Mr. Pike owned a company which mined china clay at West Creech in Dorset. The famous Blue Pool was part of his mining operations. When Mr. Pike died, Mrs. Pike became a recluse. She believed in transmigration and thought the soul of her late husband had entered a rabbit. She would allow no rabbits to be killed on the estate and paid local children half a crown for every rabbit they brought to her. The gardeners were encouraged to grow food for the rabbits; consequently the whole area was swarming with rabbits of different colours. Some of their offspring can still be seen at twilight in the grounds of the junior school – sometimes as many as thirty or forty grazing quietly between the trees. Mrs. Pike built two-storey hutches for the rabbits, enabling poachers to put a hand in the hutch and quickly grab a rabbit. During the Second World War the house was used by the Fire Service and later by the Ministry of Defence as a staff club for the De Havilland workers from Christchurch Airfield and was run by the Holiday Fellowship. At that time the grounds of the house were very overgrown and the wildlife abounded. Rabbits, of course, adders and badgers were seen in great numbers. The officers spent their evenings watching the badgers at play outside their sets which were at the present site of the junction of Holmhurst Avenue and Hinton Wood Avenue.

## BELVEDERE – WOLHAYES – MARYDALE

The estate was bounded by Braemar Drive, Hinton Wood Avenue and in the south by the Lymington Road and apart from Hoburne is probably the oldest estate in Highcliffe.

There have been two houses on this estate. The first was **Belvedere**. It was described in the Christchurch Miscellany, dated 1790, as "a neat little mansion which could be seen from the sea." According to an old map, Belvedere was built nearer to Hinton Wood Avenue than the second house which was called Wolhayes.

41

Belvedere was probably built in the 18th century and demolished at the beginning of the 20th century. It was the home of Sir William Fordyce, M.D., Lord Bute's physician. He wrote many medical books but his special interest seems to have been the use of rhubarb for medical purposes. He wrote a paper entitled *The Great Importance of Cultivating and Curing Rhubarb for Medical Uses*, for which he gained a gold award from the Society of Arts.

BELVEDERE

In 1868 Mrs. Martin, widow of the late Mr. C. Martin was in residence at Belvedere. Her daughter, Sarah Amelia, married Lord Amphlett, a lawyer and Member of Parliament, in 1880.

The next residents were Mr. and Mrs. Entwistle and their family of eight children. He was a magistrate and a school manager. Mrs. Entwistle erected a gravestone in St. Mark's churchyard to William Shaw who was coachman to Mr. Entwistle for 27 years.

**Wolhayes**, the second house, was built by the Mills family in the early part of the 20th century in the style of the White House in Washington, D.C. During the Second World War a bomb fell on the soft ground near the lake (now Lyme Crescent) and despite repeated attempts to dig it out, the bomb sank lower and lower into the mud. Eventually it was decided to leave it – as no one was likely to walk there … presumably it remains to this day.

Miss Mills was the last resident and when she died the house was bought by the Community of the Handmaids of the Sacred Heart of Jesus. The house was reopened on September 22nd 1953 as a girl's day and boarding school called 'Marydale'. Sister Bernadine, one of the teaching staff, recalls the beautiful gardens brilliant with azalea blooms, a Ha-Ha and an espalier wall. The Community was a closed order and its members were not allowed to leave the grounds except to visit the dentist. It was even necessary, at that time, to get permission from Rome if an educational visit was planned for the girls. A short distance from the house a block of sixteen classrooms was built with a gymnasium. In 1970 the Community left Highcliffe and the old house and the new buildings were demolished and the Wolhayes Garden Estate was built.

WOLHAYES

**CLIFF CLOSE**

Cliff Close was a small property between the Castle and Beacon Lodge. The grounds extended from Lymington Road to the cliff edge. It was built for Colonel Francis Adams, D.S.O., an officer in the Royal Deccan Horse, who died in 1945. It later became a hotel, 'The Cliff Close Hotel' run by Mr. and Mrs. Holden. Later it became the Galleon Public House but is now called the Hinton Oak.

## BEACON LODGE

Beacon Lodge was an estate bounded by the Lymington Road and the cliff edge. It was at one time a beacon place where a fire would be kindled to act as a signal of either an invasion or of rejoicing, as at the time of Queen Victoria's Jubilee in 1887. The fire would be allowed to burn brightly at night but would be covered during the day so as to emit dense smoke. Beacon Lodge was originally called East Highcliffe.

BEACON LODGE

Little is known of the origins of the house but it appears to have been continually leased. Amongst the tenants were: -

**General and Mrs. Orde**.
**Bishop Bloomfield**, who was Bishop of London 1828-1856.
**The Hon. Grantley Berkeley and his wife**. Grantley Berkeley was the fifth son of Earl Berkeley and a very colourful character. He fought a duel with the critic of his first book, slightly wounding him. He was the first person to propose that ladies should be allowed into the gallery of the House of Commons. He was a keen and active sportsman. At Highcliffe he taught Lord Stuart de Rothesay the art of being a country gentleman, teaching him shooting, fishing and the habits of birds, beasts and poachers.
**Sir William Goshen** rented the Lodge in 1914. Sir William had been British Ambassador in Germany.
**Sir William Gordon, Q.C.,** a Scotsman

**Major Cadbury** and his family of three boys. Residents recall the boys firing the cannon which stood near the cliff edge, frightening those who lived near. Cricket was played every day in August on the beautiful ground on the estate. It was in a very picturesque setting with a fresh green turf surrounded by trees. Residents took deckchairs and picnics to spend leisurely afternoons watching the play.

**The Co-operative Society** purchased it as a holiday hostel for their staff. It has now been demolished and the Beacon Lodge estate built.

## CULMORE HOUSE

Culmore House stood on the site now occupied by Palma and Marina Courts in Wharncliffe Road. The grounds joined those of Beacon Lodge to the west. The eastern boundary was formed by the footpath from Wharncliffe Road to the cliffs. Opposite the house was the paddock, now Elmwood Gardens.

CULMORE HOUSE

Mr. and Mrs. Power were the residents. After the death of Mrs Stuart Wortley in 1953 Mrs. Wallis-Power assumed the role of 'lady of the village'. She was tall and elegant and full of enthusiasm. From 1950 to 1952 she was Mayor of Christchurch and was a County Councillor for a longer period. Mrs. Wallis-Power was President of the Bournemouth Shakespeare Society which gave annual performances in the grounds of Culmore House. She was also a keen supporter of 'the band' as she described Bournemouth Symphony Orchestra, entertaining some of the guest artistes who are now famous names in the musical world. The R.S.P.C.A. was another charity she encouraged, becoming the National Vice President for a time. She supported the local Guides, giving generously at fund-raising events. She died while walking in the paddock. A seat in her memory was erected at the junction of Castle Avenue and Lymington Road with this inscription:

*This memorial seat was erected*
*in 1960*
*by public subscription*
*to Eileen M. Wallis-Power, J.P., C.C.*
*A devoted servant of the public and friend*
*of many worthy causes.*

## GREYSTONES

GREYSTONES

Greystones, in Waterford Road, is a house designed by E.S. Prior. It was built in 1913 for Captain and Mrs. Henry Denison. Mrs. Denison was a sister of Mrs. Stuart Wortley and Mr Denison was attached to the British Embassy in Rome. The grounds were bordered by Montagu Road, Waterford Road, Chewton Bunny and the sea. The house is built of Italian stone and decorated with a steeply pitched roof of Westmorland slates. A notable feature of the building is the tall red-bricked chimneys. In the grounds near the cliff edge (below the site of the Crow's Nest Café), was a summerhouse hung with grey tiles outside and oak panelling inside and with a balcony built over a lily pond.

The next owner, Mr. Georgie Kemp, was a sportsman who enjoyed shooting and fishing. Later Christchurch Old Peoples' Housing Society bought Greystones and under the guidance of its Secretary, the late Sir Stanley Kermode, M.B.E., it became an old peoples' home. The society later built small blocks of flats in the grounds for retired folk. In 1976 when the house needed major repairs it was closed and is now the Community Centre.

MOUNTJOY

This imposing house, Mountjoy, stood further down the lane now called Montagu Road. It was the home of the Morrisons whose son was M.P. for Salisbury.

**THE HOY**

This is the oldest house in Highcliffe, probably well over 200 years old. It is now a beautifully preserved residence in Lymington Road, opposite the junction with Castle Avenue. It is a large brick-built house, until recently thatched with barley straw but now roofed with Canadian cedar shingles. The house has been extended on both sides in keeping with the original building. On the side wall is a sealed window. It was bricked up to avoid payment of window tax. Now it has been painted to simulate a window. The house is surrounded by a concrete apron as the roof has no gutters and the rain pours off the roof onto the ground below.

In the garden are two curiously carved stones whose purpose is unknown. They may have been brought over from France by Lord Stuart de Rothesay to build the Castle.

The Hoy takes its name from the *Isle of Wight Hoy*, a boat which plied between the mainland and the Isle of Wight. In the 19th century 'Ye Olde Hoy' was one of three inns in Newtown. Gamekeepers from the estates gathered there. They brought with them their terrier dogs which fought the badger kept by the landlord. Badger baiting was a popular pastime. The gamekeepers smoked clay pipes which were smoked once then thrown away. The garden is littered with remnants of these broken pipes.

A large Russian ship was driven ashore at Chewton Bunny in the late 1830's. The Russian sailors were rescued and their baggage brought ashore to The Hoy. It is recorded that the villagers had great difficulty in making the shipwrecked seamen understand that they had hospitable intentions.

The Hoy's licence lapsed in 1868. The other inns of Newtown were the Globe and the Victoria. The Globe remains but the Victoria's licence lapsed in 1886 and the site is now occupied by the shops Lafitte Galleries, Highcliffe Coaches and Lesleys.

THE HOY

**CHEWTON MILL**

The present Mill House is about 260 years old and stands at the end of Mill Lane down in Chewton Bunny. It was a water-driven corn mill and stands on the same site as an older mill and it is still possible to see the dip made by the Mill Pond to the north of the present house. The Mill was mentioned in Chancery proceedings in the time of Elizabeth I, following a dispute when it was ruled that the Mill had always been part of the Manor of Somerford. The great mill wheel was removed by one of the owners, Miss Clutterbuck, in the late 1920's so that the wheel room could be used as a rehearsal room for the Gilbert and Sullivan productions in the village. Principal singers were hired from Bournemouth but many local people took part including Harry Lee, a local butcher, Herbie Hann, the manager of Misselbrook and Westons (later Rosencase and now G & T's), and Ken Whitcombe, the Parish sexton.

CHEWTON MILL

After General Stuart Wortley died, Mrs. Stuart Wortley lived at the Castle for a time but eventually it was sold and she retired to the Mill House where she died three years later. Half way down the footpath that runs above the Bunny towards the sea is a seat on a knoll dedicated to her memory. On the seat were the words quoted at the beginning of this book: -

*Stranger, what e'er thy colour, creed or race*
*Rest here awhile, there's virtue in this place.*

The site had been carefully selected because from that point is a superb view through the trees of the distant Isle of Wight.

## AMBERWOOD HOUSE

Amberwood House is still standing hidden behind the trees in Amberwood Gardens. It is now divided into several apartments.

The estate consisted of two parks, stretching from Ringwood Road to Thursby Road. One of the parks was used as a pasture for the cows and horses. There was a walled garden where fruit grew and a greenhouse where melons were grown. Three of the estate houses are still standing and occupied. The coachman's house has been enlarged and is now the Amberwood Inn. The gardener's cottage stands on the corner of Amberwood Drive and backs onto the railway. The dairyman's cottage, known as Amberwood Dairy Cottage stands on Cranemoor Common beside a footpath which leads to Thursby Road.

The earliest known residents of Amberwood House were the Pardoe family who had twin boys, Edward and George, who were both killed, in 1879, during the Battle of Ullandi in South Africa. There are memorials to both Edward and George in St. Mark's Church.

AMBERWOOD

The next occupant was Mrs. Mary Richmond Gayle Braddyll, a very gracious lady who spent much of her time working for charitable causes. Every evening she dressed for dinner in a beautiful silk or satin full-skirted dress decorated with bows and lace. She always wore a dainty cap made of fine lace. Mrs. Braddyll died at the age of 91 and is buried in St. Mark's churchyard.

Following the death of Mrs. Braddyll, Amberwood stood empty for some years. Rumour has it that a tramp lived in the upper part of the house and it was his carelessness which caused a fire that damaged a large part of the house.

At one time the house was bought by Sir Dan Godfrey, a musician, who was knighted for his services to municipal music. He was invited to conduct the first concert by the Bournemouth Municipal Orchestra at the old Winter Gardens in Exeter Road on May 22nd 1893. He was subsequently to become the Orchestra's Musical Director.

One of the staff of the Amberwood who recalls the house in its heyday is Mrs. Withers. She was employed at Amberwood House from 1915 to 1929 and has a fascinating story to tell of life 'below stairs'. At that time it was owned by Mrs. Braddyll who was respectfully known to the maids as the 'Missus'. Mrs. Withers was engaged as a kitchen maid whilst still in her early teens and progressed to more responsible work. She was one of five servants employed at Amberwood; there was a lady's maid, a parlour maid, a housemaid, a cook and Mrs Withers was known as the 'tweeny maid'. The workers took great pride in their work and had a real affection for the 'Missus'.

The maids rose at seven o'clock every morning. The house had to be cleaned and dusted and the grates set before breakfast at eight o'clock. After breakfast the servants attended 'Prayers' and a Bible reading. Each maid then had her own specific duties. The parlour maid cleaned the silver and arranged the flowers. The tweeny maid did the washing, prepared the vegetables, filled the oil lamps and trimmed the wicks. At ten o'clock the mistress then came down to the kitchen to discuss the day's menu with the cook. The menu was then written on a slate.

After lunch the maids were allowed time to themselves but this time was usually spent sewing the calico into nightdresses, which had been given to them by the mistress at Christmas. The wage, which the maids received in the early 1920's, was £7 per annum – paid quarterly. Most of their wages had to be spent on shoes and shoe repairs. The maids all wore uniform whilst at work. In the morning they wore blue striped print dresses but changed in the afternoon into black dresses with high collars decorated with white embroidery. Over this they wore dainty white aprons. Little strips of white embroidered muslin were gathered to make bonnets.

The maids were allowed to go home for a week's holiday each year. They were allowed to take time off on Sundays on a rota basis; 'time off' meant going out at 2 p.m. and returning by 6 p.m.

Spring-cleaning was an annual event which involved a great deal of work. The mistress went away whilst the spring-cleaning was in progress. All the books had to be removed from the bookcases; the books were banged together two by two to remove any dust and then returned when the shelves had been cleaned. The cook made the furniture polish from an old recipe using beeswax dissolved in turpentine. Amberwood had one of the first 'vacuum' cleaners. It was a hand–powered device which required one of the maids to stand on the box and move a handle backwards and forwards while the other maid sought out the dust with a long tube.

In the years when Mrs. Withers worked at Amberwood it seemed to her that the furniture never wore out or needed to be renewed. The dining room furniture was of heavy dark oak carved by a craftsman. The table linen was always of spotless white damask, and it was set with beautiful silver and glass.

In the kitchen was the usual large range. The larder was always well stocked with hanging game on which she remembers seeing maggots.

The maid's bedrooms were at the top of the house. From her bedroom window Mrs. Withers could see Studland Bay. The house was heated by coal fires and lit by oil lamps. The lamps were suspended from the ceiling on pulleys so that they could be lowered and raised easily but little oil lamps were used in order to move about the house after dark.

Although in present times the Trades Unions might have a great deal to say about the inequity of the system which prevailed during Mrs. Wither's time at Amberwood House, she found it a fulfilling experience. Many of the problems which confront workers today were insignificant as far as she was concerned, as her employer provided food, shelter and warmth. Mrs. Richmond Gayle Braddyll took a personal interest in her staff, even to the extent of providing the wedding dress when they were married.

# Chapter Six

# THE CHURCHES

There are four churches in Highcliffe, the oldest of which is the Parish Church of St. Mark's. In 1838 a small mission church was built on a field called Nundy Cole. This building has since served the village well, first as a church, then a school, a community centre and now as a youth centre. Rev. Dobson was appointed as priest-in-charge with a stipend of £140 a year plus £20 for the keep or the hire of a horse.

The nearest church, apart from the Newtown Mission Church, was Christchurch Priory. It was to the Priory that the owners of the Castle travelled each Sunday to occupy the family pew which was a timbered structure built into one of the stone arches.

Newtown developed quickly from a few houses to a village. Lord Stuart de Rothesay decided that it was against his principle of rest for man and beast to travel the four miles into Christchurch each Sunday. He donated a field known as Lodge Close for the building of a church for Newtown. The field was close to the Castle lodge gates and would be easily accessible from the Castle. Lord Stuart de Rothesay headed the building fund by giving £1,000 capital to provide a stipend of £40 per year for the priest. The foundation stone was laid on April 14th 1841 and the building was completed in 1842 at a cost of £1,464 4s. 3d. and was consecrated on January 27th 1843 by Bishop Dr. Sumner. Lord Stuart de Rothesay was away in St. Petersberg at that time and so he was represented by his two daughters, Louisa, Lady Waterford and Charlotte, Lady Canning. The service was very long lasting more than three hours.

In a letter to her parents Lady Canning describes the service of dedication: -

"I shall have so much to write to you from here that it is best to begin betimes and I hope Papa will let this letter do for him too, for you will both like to hear all about the consecration. It was yesterday and it went off to admiration. I came from Heron Court on Wednesday to make preparations and left all our establishment here and yesterday we came betimes in the morning to receive the Bishop. He came straight from Bisterne, which he consecrated on Thursday, he brought with him Dr. Dealtry and his son John, as Chaplain. He had besides an apparitor and a registrar, but who they were and where he put them I never heard, but they had things to do in the Church.

His arrival began ill, for the hall door would not open and the vestibule door afterwards stuck too, but both were remedied in time and you would have been distressed to find that the wrong chairs were carried down to the church when a message was sent up for some, those with the deer-skin bottoms, not at all appropriate. However, when we got to the Church it was thronged and no little wrong details could be perceived. Canning and I walked and the Bishop arrived at 11.00 a.m. at the great door in his carriage. Seventeen of the Clergy were there in their gowns on the benches in the Chancel, benches were just everywhere and I think Mr. Burrows in all gave 300 tickets.

The service was very long indeed, more than three hours. You would have admired a papistical procession down the middle and up again. An official somebody of the Bishop's, carrying a silver thing, presumably his pastoral staff, then he himself with a great book reading alternate verses with the congregation, the Psalm, Be Ye Lift Up Ye Everlasting Doors, etc., and all the Clergy following, some black some white. The Christchurch choir sang, the Bishop preached indifferently, although, of course, no one said so, I held one plate and Canning the other and we collected £47 6s. 10d. The Bishop gave £10, Sir George Rose £10 and Canning and I £5 each, so we had to thank the congregation for a great deal. All the poor gave pennies, sixpences and even shillings. One poor labourer gave two shillings, but I am sorry to say that I have since heard that he is wrong in the head.

The best tent was put up in the Churchyard, but the prayers were all in Church and it was not used. I made Burrows invite all the Clergy and their families to luncheon and Sir George helped to do the same with the laity and 47 people came here. Happily Mrs. Cunningham had, with great zeal, prepared a feast and we had a table for twenty in the dining room and two little tables for five each at the vestibule end of it and one for five was improvised at the other end and the last ate from covers on their laps. Mrs. Farr came to the feast but not to prayer, Mr. Farr the same but brought £1 which I thought handsome. William – Dear Fellow – sat through the Service and gave ten shillings, Lady and Miss Rose came to the prayer but not to the feast. Mrs. Barclay the reverse. Grantley was away. Hopkins, Spicer, Lord Sheffield and Mr. Wood, Clergy with wives, sisters and friends and I forgot how many more came. Keppells, a Miss Richards, a Miss Carnack from Lymington, etc., etc. Thirteen dishes of aside, an orange tree and two vases of camellias and evergreens on the table and a fair show of pies, jellies, meats, hot and cold, so you will see we kept up the honour of the house very respectably. The hall door was put in order and the Company was received in the drawing room, roaring fires but no stoves and chair covers off and the place was much admired by those of taste.

Somehow I think the Church does not meet with all the admiration it deserves. Mr. Wood, Queen's Honorary Chaplain, who is reckoned puseyite likes it very much and particularly admired the ornament by Warnell, behind the font and the fact of it being so placed."

# HIGHCLIFFE CHURCH RESTORATION ACCOUNT. 1888.
## STATEMENT OF EXPENDITURE

| | | £ | s. | d. | £ | s. | d. |
|---|---|---|---|---|---|---|---|
| 1 – Messrs. Driver & Co., Southampton, Timber Merchants. | | | | | | | |
| 866 cubic feet Pitch Pine, as per contract. | @ 2/- | 86 | 6 | 6 | | | |
| " " kiln drying | @ /3 | 4 | 10 | 6 | | | |
| 4,880 cubic feet super ditto Match-boarding | 17/- p.c. | 41 | 9 | 5 | | | |
| 10,174 feet best Slate Battens | @ 2/- | 10 | 3 | 6 | | | |
| 6 mille 20 x 10 best green Slates | @ 180/- | 54 | 0 | 0 | | | |
| 100 cubic feet Red Archangel Deal | @ 1/6. | 7 | 0 | 0 | | | |
| 2 dozen Paterm. carved to design | @ 2/- | 2 | 8 | 0 | | | |
| 190 Scaffold Boards | | 14 | 8 | 0 | | | |
| 66 Scaffold Poles | | 9 | 5 | 0 | | | |
| 20 Squares casing Boards and sundry timber | | 10 | 12 | 1 | 240 | 10 | 0 |
| 2 – Messrs. Engeert & Rolfe, London, Felt Manufacturers. | | | | | | | |
| 4,880 feet super Bitumen Felt @ /1. less 52½ p.c. | | 9 | 2 | 0 | | | |
| 288 Slabs Asphalte (for laying under timbers) | | 1 | 15 | 2 | 10 | 17 | 2 |
| 3 – Messrs. Burt & Burt. Swanage, Stone Merchants. | | | | | | | |
| 126 feet Ashlar Stone | 1/5. | 8 | 18 | 6 | | | |
| 80 feet Tooled Coping | 1/8. | 6 | 13 | 4 | 15 | 11 | 10 |
| 4 – Dunwear Brick & Tile Company. Bridgewater. | | | | | | | |
| 10,000 Bricks | | | | | 12 | 12 | 0 |
| 5 – John Brine, Christchurch. Stone Mason. | | | | | | | |
| Four Stone Corbels to pattern | | | | | 1 | 14 | 8 |
| 6 – William Pack. Newtown, Blacksmith. | | | | | | | |
| Two rolled Flitch Plates, 5¼ cwt. | | 3 | 6 | 0 | | | |
| Sundry Bolts. Plates. &c.. to order | | 14 | 19 | 10 | 18 | 5 | 10 |
| 7 – Clanton Rolfe,Esq., Oxford, Architect. | | | | | | | |
| For Advice. Working Drawings. &c. | | | | | 12 | 12 | 0 |
| 8 – T. & W. Farmiloe, London, Metal Workers. | | | | | | | |
| 13 cwt. 3qrs. 22lbs Sheet Lead | @ 14/- | | | | 9 | 15 | 3 |
| 9 – "Railway Passengers" Accident Insurance Company. | | | | | | | |
| Insurance of Workmen against all accidents | | | | | 1 | 12 | 0 |
| 10 – Good & Son. London.Rope Manufacturers | | | | | | | |
| 6 dozen Scaffold Cords. 40fms ⅜in. Rope. and | | | | | | | |
| 1 cwt. 2½in. Fall Rope | | | | | 5 | 19 | 0 |
| 11 – Winstone & Co.. London. Nail Merchants | | | | | | | |
| 3½cwt. Steel Nails | 12/- | 2 | 1 | 8 | | | |
| ¾cwt. Copper ditto | | 3 | 18 | 9 | 6 | 0 | 5 |
| 12 – Buck & Co. London.Tool Makers | | | | | | | |
| Moulding Routers. &c.. to order | | | | | 1 | 19 | 9 |
| | | | | | 337 | 9 | 11 |

| | | £ | s. | d. | £ | s. | d. |
|---|---|---|---|---|---|---|---|
| | Forward | | | | 337 | 9 | 11 |
| 13 – Chean Wood Company. London. | | | | | | | |
| Timber for Shed | | | | | 5 | 4 | 6 |
| 14 – Reeve & Co.. Stony Stratford. | | | | | | | |
| Asphalte Felt (for above Shed) | | | | | 1 | 14 | 0 |
| 15 – John Street. Christchurch. Ironmonger. | | | | | | | |
| Sundry Fittings. four Ventilators. &c. | | | | | 4 | 15 | 1 |
| 16 – Frampton & Son. Newtown. | | | | | | | |
| Two ladders to order | | | | | 1 | 14 | 6 |
| 17 – Thomas Tiller. Christchurch. | | | | | | | |
| Lime and Sand | | 7 | 17 | 1 | | | |
| Five Sacks of Cement | | 6 | 15 | 6 | | | |
| Supplying and Fixing Ridge and Cresting | | | | | 15 | 5 | 1 |
| 18 – James Brown. Chewton Farm. | | | | | | | |
| Haulage of Stone. Slate & Timber | | | | | 7 | 17 | 6 |
| 19 – James Proudlev. Hoburne Farm. | | | | | | | |
| Haulage of Timber (gratis, see Receipts) | | | | | 4 | 0 | 0 |
| 20 – S.W. Railway. – Freight of Sundries. March | | 0 | 10 | 0 | | | |
| May | | 7 | 10 | 0 | | | |
| June | | 7 | 10 | 0 | | | |
| July | | 0 | 14 | 8 | 15 | 14 | 11 |
| | | | | | 209 | 3 | 0 |
| 21 – Labour. – See separate account | | | | | | | |
| 22 – Sundry Items. – Printing and Advertising | | 0 | 17 | 6 | | | |
| Postages. Telegrams. Porterage. Chq. Books. &c. | | 1 | 17 | 8 | | | |
| 1 cwt. Sheet Lead. 16/-; ¾ cwt. Paint. 18/8. | | 1 | 10 | 8 | | | |
| Repairs to gear. 4/9.; Ridge. 6/- | | 0 | 10 | 9 | 5 | 0 | 9 |
| | Total Expenses | | | | 607 | 19 | 3 |
| Deduct Proceeds of Surplus. &c. by Private Treaty | | 21 | 11 | 0 | | | |
| " " ditto | | 12 | 5 | 0 | | | |
| " " ditto | | 30 | 1 | 6 | | | |
| " " by Public Auction | | | | | 64 | 1 | 6 |
| TOTAL ACTUAL COST OF RESTORATION | | | | | £543 | 17 | 9 |

I, the undersigned, having examined the foregoing Statement of Account, together with the various Receipts and Vouchers, hereby declare the same to be correct. Each item, including the Weekly Wages to each Man is duly signed and vouched.

Signed     HENRY STOKES

Manager, Wilts and Dorset Banking Co. Ltd.

Dated 26th October, 1888.     Christchurch Branch.

# HIGHCLIFFE CHURCH RESTORATION.

## LABOUR ACCOUNT.

| 1888 | Gallop £ s. d. | Smith £ s. d. | Ogg. £ s. d. | Barnes £ s. d. | Collis £ s. d. | Summers £ s. d. | Phippard £ s. d. | Dowding £ s. d. | Tiller £ s. d. | Cole £ s. d. | Hendy £ s. d. | Scott £ s. d. | Hiscock £ s. d. | Burt or Croucher £ s. d. | Scafflod-ers and Old Men £ s. d. | Weekly Totals £ s. d. | 1888 |
|---|---|---|---|---|---|---|---|---|---|---|---|---|---|---|---|---|---|
| Jan. 28 | 1 5 9 | | 0 7 3 | | | | | | | | | | | | | 1 13 0 | Jan. 28 |
| Feb. 4 | | | 0 2 6 | | | | | | | | | | | | | 0 2 6 | Feb. 4 |
| 11 | 0 19 0 | | | | | | | | | | | | | | | 1 13 0 | 11 |
| 18 | 1 2 6 | | 0 14 0 | | | | | | | | | | | | | 2 4 9 | 18 |
| 25 | 1 2 6 | | 1 2 3 | | | | | | | | | | | | | 1 6 6 | 25 |
| Mch. 3 | 1 4 6 | | 0 4 0 | | | | | | | | | | | | | 2 9 0 | Mch. 3 |
| 10 | 1 5 0 | 1 0 9 | 1 4 6 | | | | | | | | | | | | | 3 15 3 | 10 |
| 17 | 1 1 3 | 1 5 3 | 0 13 3 | 0 16 3 | | | | | | | | | | | | 3 8 9 | 17 |
| 24 | 1 5 3 | 1 5 3 | | 1 2 3 | | | | | | | | | | | | 4 7 6 | 24 |
| 29 | 0 19 0 | 0 19 6 | | 1 5 3 | 0 11 9 | | | | | | | | | | | 3 17 0 | 29 |
| Apl. 7 | 1 3 3 | 1 3 3 | 1 1 9 | 0 19 0 | 0 18 3 | | | | | | | | | | | 5 9 9 | Apl. 7 |
| 14 | 1 8 3 | 1 8 3 | 0 4 6 | 1 8 3 | 1 8 3 | | | | | | | | | | | 5 17 6 | 14 |
| 21 | 1 1 3 | 1 8 3 | | 1 8 3 | 1 8 3 | | | | | | | | | | | 5 6 0 | 21 |
| 28 | 1 8 3 | 1 8 3 | 1 8 3 | 1 8 3 | 0 18 3 | | | | | | | | | | | 6 11 3 | 28 |
| May 5 | 1 10 7 | 1 8 3 | 0 15 0 | 1 8 3 | 0 15 0 | | | | | | | | | | | 5 17 1 | May 5 |
| 12 | 1 10 7 | 1 8 3 | | 0 13 0 | | | | | | | | | | | | 3 16 10 | 12 |
| 19 | 1 9 6 | 1 8 3 | | 1 8 3 | 1 4 9 | | | | 0 3 0 | 0 2 0 | | | | | | 9 16 9 | 19 |
| 26 | 1 13 0 | 1 8 3 | | 1 8 3 | | | | | 1 7 0 | 0 18 0 | | 0 5 6 | | | 1 15 6 | 11 11 3 | 26 |
| June 2 | 1 13 0 | 1 8 3 | 1 8 3 | 1 8 3 | 0 15 6 | 0 5 0 | | | 1 4 9 | 0 16 6 | | 0 14 6 | 0 14 6 | 0 11 6 | 1 11 3 | 12 14 0 | June 2 |
| 9 | 1 13 0 | 1 8 3 | 0 19 9 | 1 8 3 | 1 7 9 | 1 2 6 | | | 1 7 0 | 0 14 6 | 0 18 0 | 0 12 9 | 0 15 3 | 0 12 3 | 0 12 6 | 13 4 3 | 9 |
| 16 | 1 13 0 | 1 8 3 | 1 8 3 | 1 8 3 | 1 8 3 | 1 3 6 | | | 1 7 0 | 0 18 0 | 0 15 0 | 0 14 3 | 0 15 3 | 0 11 6 | | 13 13 6 | 16 |
| 23 | 1 13 0 | 1 8 3 | 1 8 3 | 1 2 3 | 1 5 0 | 1 3 6 | 1 8 9 | | 1 9 3 | 0 19 0 | 0 18 0 | 0 15 0 | 0 15 6 | 0 12 6 | 0 15 0 | 15 13 6 | 23 |
| 30 | 1 7 5 | 1 7 0 | 1 2 0 | 1 3 6 | 0 18 0 | 0 18 0 | 4 1 14 2 | | 1 6 0 | 0 16 10 | 0 18 0 | 0 15 0 | 0 6 3 | 0 12 0 | | 13 4 6 | 30 |
| July 7 | 1 7 5 | 1 3 6 | 1 3 3 | 1 8 3 | 1 3 3 | 0 19 7 | 1 14 2 | 0 16 7 | 1 7 0 | 0 18 0 | 0 15 6 | 0 13 3 | | 0 10 9 | | 13 15 9 | July 7 |
| 14 | 1 13 0 | 1 8 3 | 1 8 3 | 1 8 3 | 1 3 3 | 1 3 6 | 1 14 2 | 1 2 4 | 1 6 6 | 0 18 0 | 0 13 0 | 0 11 8 | | | | 15 7 4 | 14 |
| 21 | 1 13 0 | 1 8 3 | 1 8 3 | 1 8 3 | 1 8 3 | 1 3 6 | 1 14 2 | 1 5 2 | 1 7 0 | 0 14 3 | 0 15 0 | 0 14 9 | 0 15 3 | | | 15 15 1 | 21 |
| 28 | 1 6 10 | 1 5 0 | 1 8 3 | 1 10 0 | 1 7 6 | 1 3 4 | 1 19 9 | 1 8 10 | 1 7 0 | | 0 17 9 | 0 15 0 | 0 10 0 | | 0 4 3 | 14 19 3 | 28 |
| Aug. 4 | | 0 12 0 | | | | | 0 18 2 | 0 6 3 | 0 12 0 | | | | | | | 2 9 5 | Aug. 4 |
| 11 | | | | | | | | 0 11 6 | | | | | | | | 0 11 6 | 11 |
| Totals. | 35 9 1 | 28 8 9 | 19 8 6 | 26 9 0 | 19 5 9 | 9 2 9 | 11 3 4 | 5 10 8 | 15 10 6 | 8 7 9 | 7 8 3 | 7 6 5 | 5 7 6 | 4 11 3 | 5 13 6 | | |
| | | | | | | | | | | | | | | | | 209 3 0 | Grand Total. |

In 1861 the first vicarage was built at the junction of Hinton Wood Avenue and Lymington Road. This was a very unsatisfactory building and was altered and adapted and finally demolished in 1966. (The houses in Abbots Close now stand on the site.)

In 1862 Highcliffe became an ecclesiastical parish but the village still retained the name of Newtown. A turret clock was bought by public subscription and erected in 1879 between the organ and the west window. Unfortunately, its tick was so loud that in 1933, when the organ was moved, the clock was removed.

The church has been altered three times: -

1867    The westward extension was built.
1888    The roof was raised.
1932    The Chancel was altered, the vestry added and the organ moved from the gallery.

It was proposed in 1906 to build a Parish Hall by public subscription and house-to-house collections were organised. The Hall, consisting of one room, a gas ring and a standpipe, was built at a cost of £1,147 11s. 7d. It is now the Public Library.

In 1954 the Benefices of Highcliffe and Hinton were united, which meant that the Vicar would be chosen alternately by Hinton and Highcliffe. The Rev. Barnett explained the system in the Parish Magazine: -

**The Advowson of Highcliffe – Change of Patron**                    **August 1961**

"When St. Mark's Church was dedicated in 1843, until 1948, the patron of the benefice of Highcliffe, that is the person with the right to appoint the Vicar, was the owner of Highcliffe Castle; originally this was Lord Stuart de Rothesay who died in 1845. For about twenty years the patron was his widow, succeeded in 1867 by her daughter Louisa, Marchioness of Waterford who died on May 12th 1891. Her heir, by bequest, was her second cousin, Major General E.M. Stuart Wortley who died in 1934. The General's son, Rothesay, had predeceased him, leaving a widow who, in her turn, became the owner of the Castle and consequently patron of the benefice. Subsequently the Castle was purchased from her by General Stuart Wortley's son-in-law, the Earl of Abingdon and, as it is well known locally, was occupied until 1948 by the General's widow, Mrs. Violet Stuart Wortley.

In 1950 the Castle was sold away from the family but the a*dvowson*, the right to appoint the Vicar, was not included in the sale. The Earl thus remained the patron, though as a Roman Catholic, he was by Act of Parliament debarred from exercising his right of appointment. This Act lays down that in such cases the right of presentation vests in the University of Oxford, by whom Mr Barnett was nominated in 1952. Earlier, in 1943, Mr. Brownlow had been appointed by the Bishop of Winchester, because on that occasion the

57

University had been unable to find a priest prepared to come here. As it is well known, the Earl of Abingdon has now disposed of his property in Highcliffe and consequently he has presented the *advowson* to the See of Winchester.

Whilst we regret this break with the family of our founder, it is clearly advantageous for the patron to be Anglican. The Bishop of Winchester thus becomes the alternate patron with Sir George Meyrick. This is because the Order of the Queen in Council dated October 1954, uniting the benefices of Highcliffe and Hinton Admiral provides *inter alia*, that the incumbents shall be appointed alternately by the patron of Highcliffe and the patron of Hinton."

The earliest Parish magazines reflect vividly the life of the village as well as that of the church. They show too, that the church was concerned for man's physical as well as his spiritual being. The following extracts from St. Mark's Church magazine illustrate the point: -

**January 19th 1856**

"The first wedding to take place at St. Mark's was that of Caroline, second daughter of Lt. Col. Cameron of Nea House, to Edward Windsor."

**December 1880**

"On Sunday last two eloquent sermons were preached in Highcliffe Church, morning and evening, by the Rev. T.A. Lindon, Vicar, and a collection made for the purpose of supplying beef and bread to the poor of the district. We are glad to say the request was nobly responded to. The contributions amounted to £9 which are being distributed to the poor who are very thankful for the liberality bestowed on them."

**March 1888 – Mothers' Meeting**

"Some have not joined the Clothing Club through a misunderstanding it seems. They have thought that it was necessary to pay in one shilling a month and that no lesser sum would be received or bring any benefit. This is quite a mistake, the Club is intended to help the poor and where any cannot afford a shilling a month they can pay less and will receive a bonus in proportion at the end of the year."

**April 1888 – The Coal Club**

"The principal subscribers to the Coal Club have been much dissatisfied with its present management and some of them met together to draw up fresh rules which will immediately come into force. They are these: -

1 The coal club is open to any parishioner whose usual earnings are not more than fifteen shillings a week with house rent to pay.

2 No member shall pay more than fifteen shillings in a year.

# WOMENS CLOTHING CLUB.

## RECEIPTS.

| 1887-8. | | £. | s. | d. |
|---|---|---|---|---|
| ug. 7 | W. E. | 2 | 0 | 0 |
| ct. 1 | Mrs. Stuart | 1 | 0 | 0 |
| 21 | Lady Waterford | 2 | 0 | 0 |
| 26 | Lady Amphlett | 1 | 0 | 0 |
| " | A. Travers. Esq. | 4 | 0 | 0 |
| 28 | Mrs. Braddyll | 1 | 0 | 0 |
| ov. 2 | Mrs. Entwisle | 2 | 0 | 0 |
| 23 | T. P. Elphinston. Esq. | 0 | 10 | 6 |
| ec. 1 | Mrs. Craufurd | 1 | 0 | 0 |
| " | F. Ricardo. Esq. | 1 | 0 | 0 |
| " | Lady Thursby | 3 | 0 | 0 |
| " | A. Ross. Esq. | 0 | 10 | 0 |
| " | Deposited by 64 members | 36 | 15 | 0 |
| | | £55 | 15 | 6 |

## PAYMENTS.

| 1887-8. | £. | s. | d. |
|---|---|---|---|
| Balance due to Treasurer | 0 | 9 | 0 |
| Payn Bros. | 30 | 6 | 0 |
| Frank Allen | 5 | 19 | 0 |
| George Allen | 11 | 18 | 0 |
| E. Small | 4 | 0 | 6 |
| Balance in hand | 3 | 3 | 0 |
| | £55 | 15 | 6 |

AMELIA AMPHLETT, Treasurer.
Examined and found correct, S. E. V. FILLEUL, March 26th, 1888

# HIGHCLIFFE BOOT AND SHOE CLUB.

## RECEIPTS.

| 1887. | | £. | s. | d. |
|---|---|---|---|---|
| ug. 7th | W. E. | 2 | 0 | 0 |
| ct. 1st | Mrs. Stuart | 1 | 0 | 0 |
| 21st | Lady Waterford | 1 | 0 | 0 |
| 26th | Lady Amphlett | 0 | 10 | 0 |
| 26th | A.Travers. Esq. | 1 | 0 | 0 |
| 28th | Mrs. Braddyll | 0 | 10 | 0 |
| ov. 2nd | Mrs. Entwisle | 1 | 0 | 0 |
| 24th | T. P. Elphinston. Esq. | 0 | 10 | 6 |
| " | Mrs. Craufurd | 0 | 10 | 0 |
| ct 29th | Deposited by 65 Scholars | 13 | 5 | 9 |
| | | £21 | 6 | 3 |

## EXPENDITURE.

| 1887. | | £. | s. | d |
|---|---|---|---|---|
| Nov. 1st | Balance due to Treasurer | 1 | 7 | 7 |
| Oct. 29th | Froud Bros. | 17 | 5 | 6 |
| " " | Allen (Purewell) | 1 | 0 | 8 |
| " " | Head | 0 | 12 | 10 |
| Nov. 9th | Froud Bros. | 0 | 5 | 3 |
| | Balance in hand | 0 | 14 | 5 |
| | | £21 | 6 | 3 |

H. ELLWOOD, Secretary.
Examined and found correct, S. E. V. FILLEUL, March 26th, 1888

# COAL CLUB ACCOUNT.

## RECEIPTS.

| 1887. | | £. | s. | d. |
|---|---|---|---|---|
| ug. 7 | W. E. | 1 | 0 | 0 |
| ct. 21 | Lady Waterford | 5 | 0 | 0 |
| 26 | A. Travers. Esq. | 2 | 0 | 0 |
| | Lady Amphlett | 1 | 0 | 0 |
| 30 | General Stuart | 5 | 0 | 0 |
| ov. 2 | Mrs. Entwisle | 6 | 0 | 0 |
| | Mrs. Braddyll | 3 | 0 | 0 |
| 24 | T. P. Elphinston. Esq. | 1 | 0 | 0 |
| 25 | Mrs. Craufurd | 1 | 0 | 0 |
| ec. 6 | F. Ricardo. Esq. | 2 | 0 | 0 |
| 22 | General Maberly | 1 | 10 | 0 |
| 1888. | | | | |
| an. 3 | Colonel Surman | 3 | 0 | 0 |
| 9 | J. D. Gibb. Esq. | 3 | 0 | 0 |
| | | £34 | 10 | 0 |

## PAYMENTS.

| 1887. | | £. | s. | d |
|---|---|---|---|---|
| Dec. 26 | Balance due to Treasurer | 0 | 11 | 9 |
| | 13 tons. 15 cwt. Coal. Co-oper-ative Society | 11 | 8 | 2 |
| 1888. | | | | |
| Jan. 3 | Troke. distributing ditto | 3 | 0 | 0 |
| Jan. 25 | J Lake. 9 cwt. | 0 | 9 | 0 |
| Feb. 25 | J Lake. 13 tons. 7 cwt. | 13 | 7 | 0 |
| Mar. 26 | J Lake. 5 tons. 9 cwt. | 5 | 9 | 0 |
| April 1 | Balance in hand | 0 | 5 | 1 |
| | | £34 | 10 | 0 |

S. E. V. FILLEUL, Treasurer.
Examined and found correct, E. H. BELLAIRS, March 26th, 1888

59

3    A bonus of sixpence in the shilling will be allowed to the members.

4    Payments will be received at Amberwood on the second and fourth Mondays of the month between ten and eleven o'clock in the morning. Mrs. Braddyll of Amberwood has kindly undertaken to be the Secretary."

## July 1888 – Typhoid Fever hits the Village

"The Vicar was taken to Boscombe Infirmary. My last stay at Boscombe Infirmary has been terribly saddened by the death of the last victim of the fever. I hoped that with the excellent treatment and care of this Hospital, Rose Edmund might have pulled through, but she seemed to have no constitution or power to rally and just as our hopes were rising by the lessening of the fever, she sank through an infection of the lungs. Her death was quite sudden. She lay in a ward at the opposite end of the passage to myself. The same nurses went to and fro between us and I constantly enquired about her condition. She had required very much attention and I was surprised one night when the nurses seemed so much at liberty. They tried to hide the fact of her death from me.

I said to the nurse, 'Rose seems very quiet now.' The nurse said, 'Yes, she is very quiet.' I said again, 'I hope then she is doing better now.' 'No', said the nurse, 'she is not better.' I questioned a little more and found that my poor fellow sufferer was gone and that I was left alone. It seems hard to realise that she will never again be at her class in the Sunday School. So lately she was busy about my house and she will never be there again.

It comes most solemnly home to me the one should be taken and the other left. I read to myself the burial service at the hour of the funeral at Highcliffe. Rose Edmond, aged 18 years, was laid to rest at Highcliffe on June 20th 1888."

## November 1888

"I am publishing this month the present statement of our offertory fund, the last account appeared in the May magazine. I do it because the grumbling reaches my ears from the poor, that they don't get as much money given to them from the Church, as they did in former times. Naturally enough, they blame me for it as they do when they don't get as much beef or coals, etc., as they expected. Of course, the reason that they receive this is that there is less collected to give away.

It will be seen from this balance sheet that there is actually a deficit at the moment of just £4. Out of nothing comes nothing, the bag is so empty because no alms were collected in the Summer when we had the services in the Reading Room but apart from that, not as much is collected in Church in the monthly offertories as is given away by myself and the church wardens. This is not because there are less collections for the poor than there used to be. In fact we have been having one collection a month more for this object. As our finances were in this state and the deficit increasing, we settled that the fairest way of bringing them square again was to reduce the regular weekly payments by one half and thus divide the burden equally amongst us all. This will have to continue for a few weeks until we are right again. I do not like to hear these grumbles, least of all do I like to have it said amongst you that I rob the poor, so I publish again the accounts of the offertory fund and I take this opportunity of warning the discontented that the certain result of their conduct will be that the charities of the parish will be less kindly supported than they have been. People do not like their gifts to be received ungratefully and when they are doing so much there should be no grumbles."

## January 1889

"250lbs. of beef were given away to the poor this Christmas. The Highcliffe Boot and Shoe Club stood at £20 17s. 4d. of which £13 2s. 1d. had been deposited by the children.

There was also the Highcliffe Women's Clothing Club and the amount in that was £56 2s. 11d."

## March 1889

"The Coal Club accounts are published this month, altogether close upon 62 tons of coal have been distributed. This has been of real good quality such as could not have been bought by members at less than 21 shillings a ton. It has cost them 10 shillings a ton, thus the members of the Club have good cause to thank the subscribers who have enabled them to procure it so cheaply."

## April 1891

"At the Easter Vestry Meeting it was noticed that the behaviour of children at the back of the Church had much improved and thanks were given to Mr.Skinner to whose presence among them it was due. It was noticed as a cause for congratulation and thankfulness that the language of the elder boys and children in the village was very much improved since last year."

No great events of significance to this narrative took place between 1891-1961.

## January 1962 – The Selfridge Graves

"For many years the graves have been untended and have gradually become more unkempt. It is good to know, therefore, that as a result of an approach by the Vicar, Messrs. Selfridge propose, in future, making an annual payment to the Parochial Church Council for the maintenance of the graves."

## ST. MARK'S CHURCH

**August – September 1963**

"Lady Lorraine, daughter of the late Hon. Mrs. E.M. Stuart Wortley, formerly of Highcliffe Castle, has recently given to the Parish a photograph of St. Mark's Church taken in or about 1870. This photograph is of considerable historic interest showing the Church as it was after the westward extension of 1867, but before the raising of the roof in 1888, and the enlarging of the chancel and vestry in 1932. It is also interesting to see but one grave on the northern side of the Church, that of the Vicar's infant son, who died in 1869. Lady Lorraine has also presented to the Red House Museum several early photographs of Highcliffe Castle."

**December 1966 – The Sale of the Vicarage**

"The nett proceeds of the sale of the old Vicarage and a small portion of the adjacent church lands amounted to around £22,500, of this sum about £4,000 is available towards the building of our new Church Hall."

**February 1970**

"The Borough Council has now decided that the War Memorial shall remain in its present position, but has also expressed willingness to accept responsibility for the future maintenance of the memorial and its immediate surrounds."

## THE METHODIST CHURCH

The first Primitive Methodist Chapel was built in Highcliffe in 1908 but before that time groups of Methodists used to meet in the home of John and Jane Frampton. As this house group increased in numbers, they became a Society of the Methodist Church. This Society raised most of the money for the Chapel to be built in Highcliffe at a cost of £683 14s. 8d. The first Service was held in the Chapel on Sunday, June 8th 1908.

HIGHCLIFFE METHODIST CHURCH

The Chapel seated between eighty and ninety people, it had one other room which served as vestry, schoolroom and kitchen. Pastoral care was exercised by ministers from the Bournemouth Circuit and by retired ministers in the district.

John Frampton owned property in Lymington Road. His home was called Grace Villa – this is now Bertie's Fish and Chip shop. He gave the adjoining piece of land to the Methodist Church. His business premises, 'John Frampton Motor and Cycle Works' is now Highcliffe Garage. In 1928 John Frampton made a gift of £2,800 to the Chapel. The money was invested and according to his wishes was to be used for the enlargement of the Church and towards a Minister's stipend. The Frampton Trust still brings an income to the Methodist Church in Highcliffe.

In 1939 Mr. and Mrs. Frampton celebrated their Diamond Wedding Anniversary and the members of the Chapel presented a Communion Table, suitably inscribed, to commemorate the event. The Communion Table is still in use in the Church vestibule.

The following report in the *Christchurch Times* of June 3rd 1939 not only reports the Diamond Wedding but also throws an interesting sidelight on the development of the village.

### Diamond Jubilee of Mr. and Mrs. Frampton

"The happiest married pair in Highcliffe this week is Mr. and Mrs. John Frampton, of Grace Villa, who celebrated on Wednesday last their Diamond Wedding. Mr. Frampton, who may be described as virtually the founder of Highcliffe as it is today, and his wife, are among the best known and respected residents of the village, and numerous wishes for their happiness and continued long life have been received; but what is especially treasured is a greeting from Their Majesties the King and Queen.

At the age of 81 (he will be 82 next December, and his wife a year younger), Mr. Frampton is still an energetic gardener. He attends the little Methodist Church, to which his later years have been dedicated, with regularity and unabated enthusiasm. Both Mr. and Mrs. Frampton are enjoying the best of health, despite their years.

Married at Kingston Church, Portsmouth, on May 28th 1879, Mr. and Mrs. Frampton have by dint of grit, perseverance and hard work, won through life's battles until at the celebration of this happy anniversary it would be difficult to find a happier or more devoted pair.

### Progenitors of Modern Highcliffe

The statement that Mr. Frampton and his wife were the progenitors of modern Highcliffe is no idle one. Mr Frampton's life history begins as one of 16 children born to Mr. James Frampton, a builder, who lived in Lone Tree Cottage, then known as Victoria House, Highcliffe. In those days there were no shops – not even a Post Office, and the postman, when he did visit the village, blew a whistle to apprise the inhabitants of the 18 houses of his presence.

Highcliffe housewives baked their own bread because there was no bakery. There were no butchers and, of course, no grocers. St. Mark's Church was in the course of construction. One of Mr. Frampton's earliest recollections is the public festivities in the village when King Edward VII became Prince of Wales. On this occasion a fête was held in the grounds opposite the Vicarage and Mr. Frampton's father built for the occasion some roundabouts, the motive power for which was supplied by two men turning a driving wheel.

Mr. Frampton left school before he was nine years old and went to work in a carpenter's shop where he remained until he was fifteen."

When the Methodist Chapel celebrated its Golden Jubilee in 1958 there was clearly a need for a larger church and more appropriate premises for the weekday activities. A Gift Day was held as part of the Jubilee Thanksgiving Celebrations and the new building was started four years later. The new Church and ancillary buildings, designed by John Pantlin of Wimborne, were finally completed in 1963, during the ministry of the Rev. Gregory Carter. The Church was opened and dedicated by Rev. Reginald Stonham who, at that time, was Chairman of the District. The total building programme cost £30,000.

## THE CHURCH OF THE HOLY REDEEMER

THE CHURCH OF THE HOLY REDEEMER

There was no Roman Catholic Parish of Highcliffe until 1969. Before this time Catholics attended worship at either Christchurch or New Milton Catholic Churches. In 1953 the Congregation of the Sons of the Immaculate Heart of Mary, or the Claretian Missionaries, purchased Highcliffe Castle. They were a modern religious order and Highcliffe Castle became a seminary for the training of missionaries. The Claretians generously opened their Chapel in the Great Hall of the Castle as a Mass Centre for the villagers. The Claretians only stayed in Highcliffe for twelve years. When they left in 1965 the village was, once more, without a Catholic Church.

However, the house, Wolhayes, was now Marydale Convent and the teaching sisters of The Handmaids of the Sacred Heart of Jesus allowed their new gymnasium to be used on Sundays as a Mass Centre. When the Convent was demolished the sisters donated one acre of the grounds, a corner of the hockey field, for the people of Highcliffe to build a Catholic Church. On July 12th, 1969 the Church in Kilmington Way was opened and dedicated by the Bishop of Portsmouth. The Church was designed as a multi-purpose building. The altar can be partitioned off when the building is not used for worship.

## CRANEMOOR UNITED REFORM CHURCH

Cranemoor, originally a Congregational Chapel, stands on a large site in Ringwood Road. Behind the church is a well-kept garden and from an old map it seems that the original site included the land on which the bungalows on the north side of Pinewood Close now stand.

The beginnings of the 'cause', as it was known in the early days, have been difficult to trace; but from documents in the Dorset Archives it may be assumed that there was an earlier meeting place which appears to have been in Hinton as it was outside the Highcliffe ecclesiastical parish. The following extract from one of the church's documents confirms this: -

"October 1st 1825

A certain building situate in the Parish of Christchurch in the occupation of Nicholas Verge is set apart by a congregation of His Majesty's Protestant subjects dissenting from the Church of England and for a place of Public Worship and Service of Almighty God.

*Signed:* C. Wooldridge
Deputy Registrar"

The building, referred to above, was a house and as the 'cause' prospered it became necessary to make alterations to the building. A wall was knocked down to make two small rooms into one large room.

One of the earliest pioneers of the 'cause' in Walkford was Henry Abbott of Christchurch, who was joined in 1828 by William Lane who wrote in his diary, dated 1858: -

"One source of much regret we have is the continued illness of my long tried and much valued helper, Henry Abbott: our fellowship was pleasant and without interruption for nearly 30 years and we fell not out by the way."

The site of the present church was given by Mr. Bramble of Gore Farm. Originally it had been planned to build a church and a cottage and also to provide a burial ground but the ground was never used for the latter purpose. There was no money available to build at that time until Jesse Hall had a serious accident. It was a strange story. Mr. Jesse Hall, of Burton, met with a gunshot wound at Waterditch and realized he would never recover. On his deathbed he bequeathed his money to the dissenting people of Walkford for the purpose of erecting a church. There is no memorial tablet to Mr. Jesse Hall in the Church because …

"…..it was the great aversion held by the Rev. Daniel Gunn to any such tablet being placed on the walls of places of worship, as being too much identified with the chapels to the saints found in Roman Catholic Churches."

CRANEMOOR CHAPEL

In 1972 the Congregational Church united with the Presbyterian Church and the two became the United Reform Church. Cranemoor is part of the Christchurch Group of the United Reform Church which includes the churches at Burton and Somerford and the main church in Millhams Street, Christchurch.

The Hall was built at the rear of the church in 1975 and since then the church has been decorated and refurbished, including an electric organ, lectern, font and chairs to replace the old pews.

# Chapter Seven

# ST. MARK'S JUNIOR MIXED SCHOOL 1844-1900

The school building in Lymington Road, opposite the Recreation Ground, has played a significant part in the life of the village for more than 140 years. It was built on a field called Nundy Cole which was given to the village by Mr. John Spicer of Somerford Grange. A small lecture room was built there in 1837 and, later, the Newtown Mission Church. Written into the original deeds of the property was the clause that if the building was not used for divine worship for a period of twelve months it was to be used as a school for the poor of Highcliffe. St. Mark's Church had been built and the Newtown Mission Church was no longer needed. The school was opened in 1844. The schoolmistress was Miss Belbin, the 'daughter of a highly respectable Christchurch brick-layer'. The School House was built in 1856.

Most voluntary schools at this time were run on Church principles but received a grant from the government towards maintaining the premises and were called National Schools. St. Mark's Church of England Mixed School came into this category. The school was visited regularly once a year by an inspector appointed by the Education Authority and the size of the monetary grant to the school depended on the inspector's report. Money towards the running of the school was donated by local gentry and the children contributed one penny a week. The Vicar and Managers of the school kept a close watch on the school, visiting regularly and questioning the children on the work they had learnt. Another visitor to the school was the Diocesan inspector who examined the children in religious knowledge. The children were tested in Old and New Testament knowledge, Catechism and Liturgy and Repetition.

The children came from the four villages of Newtown, Chewton, Walkford and Guss. It was the teacher's statutory duty to keep the School Log, a record of the daily happenings of the school. The following are excerpts from the earliest School Logs: -

**1867**

July   26  Very wet today and a thin school in consequence.
Aug.   12  The summer holidays commenced today. They will continue for two to three weeks.
Sept.   9  A circus in Christchurch drew off most of the children.
       24  Made a rule not to keep the school doors open after half past nine and half past two.
Oct.    2  School Treat at Hoburne.

    4 Punished several children for going into the wood at dinner time.

**1868**

April 28 Smallpox at Guss.

May   1 Some of the children went into the churchyard and ran about the graves. J.H. threw stones at the bell. He was ordered to return the prize he got for good conduct.

    18 52 children attended.

    20 Sent home four children as smallpox was in their immediate neighbourhood.

    22 Seven boys drowned at beach whilst bathing.

June   2 Ordered: -   6 dozen copy books
                        2 boxes slate pencils
                        1 bottle black ink
                        1 box pens
                        36 dozen pen holders

July   2 Several children have whooping cough.

    20 Children asked leave to go harvesting.

    22 Monitor's desk has had a lock and key put on it. The rule that school money should be paid every week is to be strictly enforced.

Nov.   2 Shoe Club opened today with 60 members and shoes distributed.

**1869**

Jan.   12 Employed two monitors at 6d. per week.

    20 This is the second week of the Highcliffe Soup Kitchen next to the School

Feb.   1 Two children sent home with measles.

Mar.   3 H.D. is wanted at home to keep cows.

Apr.   19 Standard 1     12 pupils
                2        7 pupils
                3       9 pupils
                4       3 pupils
                5       5 pupils
                6      22 pupils

Apr.   20 Cautioned boys not to rob birds' nests.

May   12 Rev. Aitkin visited the school. He was told that A.G. had misconducted herself in church on Sunday morning. She was sent out of church.

    13 Paper had been used instead of slate for dictation.

    27 School is thin because of the Christchurch Fair.

July   8 Gen. Stuart called and paid the teacher his part of the teacher's salary (£5).

12 Gen. Stuart called to say the children made a noise going into church on Sunday.

Aug. 12 Annual Day and Sunday School treat given by Lady Waterford and Hon. Mrs. Stuart at Highcliffe.

Sept. 24 A.S. will soon leave school to work with his grandfather.

Nov. 29 Mrs. Aitkin's soup was given to all the children. (Continued on and off).

Dec. 24 Rebecca Gibbs, a pupil, died.
William Frampton, a pupil, died.

Passing of the Education Act 1870 compelled all children to attend school from 5 to 13 years. Parents had to contribute 6d. – 9d. a week. There were two kinds of schools National Schools run by the Church (as St. Mark's) and Board Schools run by a board of managers, where religious denominational teaching was prohibited.

**1870**

Feb. 14 W.W. punished for loitering.

Mar. 10 Kept all in till 5 o'clock for singing lesson.

May 26 E.L. has gone into service with Mrs. Tucker.
27 Landers man came to peg out ground for new classroom.

June 1 New chimney pot on front room chimney.
16 Received £35 2s. 3d. Government Grant to 31st March 1870 from Rev. Aitkin.
23 Cautioned children about going into Mr. Entwhistle's field and to the shore.

Aug. 11 Annual Treat given by Lady Waterford at the Castle.
Two children absent – gleaning.

**1871**

Jan. Rev. Aitkin appears to visit the school each day.

Aug. 10 School broke for four weeks – harvesting.

Sept. 22 Engaged two monitors to officiate for the pupil teacher who comes in six months time. Salary 1 shilling a week.

**1872**

April 12 William James Forster, pupil teacher, started.
19 Fred Gregory, in examination schedule, died from Bronchitis.

May 31 Eliza Reed and Fanny Reed died of Scarlet Fever.

Nov. 29 Children ill with mumps.

# HIGHCLIFFE NATIONAL SCHOOLS.
## Annual Balance for the Year ending 30th April 1891.

### RECEIPTS.

| | £. | s. | d. | £. | s. | d. |
|---|---|---|---|---|---|---|
| nt from Education Depart- | | | | | | |
| t o/a 1890. | | | | 89 | 8 | 4 |
| e subscription and dona- | | | | | | |
| s o/a ditto | 6 | 0 | 0 | | | |
| bscriptions o/a School Year 1891: - | | | | | | |
| isa, Marchioness of | | | | | | |
| terford [the late] | 30 | 0 | 0 | | | |
| . and Mrs. Stuart | 30 | 0 | 0 | | | |
| John Thursby, Bart. | 15 | 0 | 0 | | | |
| y Amphlett | 5 | 0 | 0 | | | |
| s. Entwhistle. | 5 | 0 | 0 | | | |
| ur Entwhistle, Esq., J.P. | 5 | 0 | 0 | | | |
| itto          donation | 1 | 0 | 0 | | | |
| s Martin | 5 | 0 | 0 | | | |
| . and Mrs. Bellairs | 3 | 0 | 0 | | | |
| rs Braddyll (half - year) | 1 | 10 | 0 | | | |
| . Elphinston. Esq. | 2 | 0 | 0 | | | |
| or. F. H. D. Eyre | 1 | 0 | 0 | | | |
| milton Fletcher, Esq. | 3 | 3 | 0 | | | |
| t. B.H. Holme. | 3 | 0 | 0 | | | |
| P.  Latham, Esq. (half yr.) | 1 | 11 | 6 | | | |
| . Maberly, C.B. | 2 | 0 | 0 | | | |
| icardo, Esq. | 3 | 0 | 0 | | | |
| . A.D. and Mrs. Ryder | 3 | 0 | 0 | | | |
| Ross | 0 | 2 | 6 | | | |
| | | | | 125 | 7 | 0 |
| ection in Church | | | | 3 | 16 | 3 |
| ool Pence | | | | 20 | 16 | 3 |
| e of Work, & c. | | | | 8 | 15 | 1 |
| ance as at 30th April, 1891 | | | | | | |
| nished the Education De- | | | | | | |
| tment | | | | 90 | 15 | 9 |
| | | | | £338 | 18 | 8 |

### EXPENDITURE.

| | £. | s. | d | £. | s. | d |
|---|---|---|---|---|---|---|
| Balance due to Teacher | | | | | | |
| o/a of 1890 | | | | 89 | 8 | 4 |
| Salaries for School year 1891 | | | | | | |
| Teacher | 120 | 0 | 0 | | | |
| Assistants | 75 | 6 | 5 | | | |
| Monitor | 1 | 6 | 0 | | | |
| | | | | 196 | 12 | 5 |
| Books and Stationery | | | | 19 | 2 | 10 |
| Fuel, Light and cleaning | | | | 17 | 18 | 4 |
| New Furniture and Repairs | | | | 11 | 3 | 1 |
| Fire Insurance | | | | 0 | 7 | 6 |
| Other Expenses | | | | 4 | 6 | 2 |
| | | | | £338 | 18 | 8 |

*Items belonging to the above year, and received subsequent to balance (which had to be struck in accordance with regulations of Education Department).*

| | £. | s. | d. | £. | s. | d. |
|---|---|---|---|---|---|---|
| vernment grant for School | | | | | | |
| r ending 30th April, 1891 | | | | 77 | 14 | 6 |
| e Subscriptions - | | | | | | |
| s Bradyll (half-year) | 1 | 10 | 0 | | | |
| . Latham | 1 | 11 | 6 | | | |
| tto        donation | 1 | 0 | 0 | | | |
| Ross | 0 | 2 | 6 | | | |
| | | | | 4 | 4 | 0 |
| ual deficit on the year | | | | 8 | 17 | 3 |
| | | | | £90 | 15 | 9 |

| | £. | s. | d |
|---|---|---|---|
| Balance brought down | 90 | 15 | 9 |
| | £90 | 15 | 9 |

Signed, 6th June, 1891,          E.H. BELLAIRS, Secretary and Treasurer.

Audited with Vouchers and found correct,          B. H. HOLME

**1873**

Feb.    15  Received notice from the Council Offices to say that the school year will finish April 30th instead of March 31st.

Aug.    9  The Master leaves by notice from Gen. Stuart.

Sept.  25  Monitors have their lessons between 1 and 2 p.m.

Oct.    15  There are many children of dissenting parents who are not allowed to attend Catechism lessons.

          28  Many children are unable to attend for the want of boots.

Nov.   14  The Shoe Club was started again, membership extended to all the children in the neighbourhood.

The earliest Inspector's Reports of St. Mark's School date from 1875 when John Vickers was appointed as a Pupil Teacher. The school managers were responsible for the pupil teacher receiving the correct amount of instruction from the teacher. At the end of a year they had to certify that such instruction had been carried out. From time to time the Managers had to attend during the instruction of the Pupil Teacher. The average attendance of children during 1875 was twenty five children under 6 years of age and seventy nine over 6 years of age. The eldest child was about 13 years old. The school was given a satisfactory report at the end of this year.

During the next three years (1876 - 1879) the number of children attending increased and each year the school was given a satisfactory report by the Inspector, thus ensuring the continuation of the government grant which at this time was about £70. There were one or two interesting comments from the Reports: -

1876        More apparatus required.

1878        Children are very tidy and well behaved.

1879        The Third Standard is very weak but great pains have been bestowed on the needlework.

The Headmaster continues to record daily the school activities in the School Log: -

**1876**

Sept.  28  Attendance low – tea party at Cranemoor Chapel for the children who attend on Sunday.

Dec.    8  At 11.30 the girls were marched from the school to Highcliffe Castle to each receive a red winter cloak.

**1877**

Sept.  14  Many children potato picking.

Nov.   28  Lady Waterford complained that some pillow cases made in the school had some very large stitches.

**1878**

Jan.    22   Several children are tapping for Sir George Meyrick.

July   30   By the kindness of Lady Waterford, the children belonging to the Day
and Sunday Schools and the members of the choir were taken to the
Forest, near Holmsley Station, and thoroughly enjoyed themselves.
A capital tea was served to them under the trees, after which there was
cricket, dancing to the music of a band engaged for the day, and races
in sacks, etc. At about 7-7.30 p.m. all were assembled to start home.
No accident occurred. The wagons were kindly lent for the occasion by
Messrs. Pack, Proudley and Brown. Mr. Lane's (Christchurch) apparatus
for boiling water and making tea were much approved.
Lady Waterford and guests attended to the wants of the children at
tea-time and in various ways entertained them afterwards.

**1879**

Mar.  27   Some of the boys went down to Mr. Entwhistles' field at dinner time to
catch young rabbits. They dug some out of a burrow and W.H. put them
in his bag with the intention of carrying them home but was prevented
by some of his colleagues.

May        John Vickers finished his engagement as Pupil Teacher, but retained as
assistant master, with no increase in salary.

June    3   School closed. At the "Globe Inn" a few yards from the school, a fête is
held every Tuesday in Whitsun Week in connection with the Benefit
Clubs in the district.
These fêtes are certainly very unfit for children to attend – so the school
is closed and school children are recommended to keep away from the
immediate neighbourhood of the Globe.

June  28   John Vickers accepted an appointment in a Boys' School.

Aug.   13   School Treat. The children assembled at the school at 1.30 and preceded
by the Hordle Brass Band marched to Highcliffe arriving there at 2.30
p.m. After presenting flowers to Lady Waterford the children were taken
to the cliffs to play. At 3 p.m. again marched to the House to have their
tea in the Entrance Hall. After tea, games were again played on the cliffs
till 6.30, when each child was presented with an orange and a bun by
Lady Waterford at the Hall door, and then there were three hearty cheers
for Lady Waterford.

Dec.    5   The weather has been very cold all week. Several children cannot get
their boots on for chilblains, others are ill with chickenpox.

**1880**

Mar.1    Measles very prevalent. Attendance low. It is unfortunate for me (the teacher) that I am partner in the school (i.e. so far as pence and grants are concerned).

April 2    Heavy rain – attendance 21 – the prospects are certainly not very encouraging to a teacher who depends upon the grant for the larger proportion of his income.

Aug. 11    Children absent at Bournemouth for the opening of the new pier.

ST. MARK'S SCHOOL
(Now the Highcliffe Youth Centre)

In 1881, it is reported that the premises were enlarged and much improved. The tone of the annual Inspector's Report in 1883 changes and becomes rather pedantic: -

"The infants are in a backward state, throughout the school penmanship is weak, not as satisfactory as it might be. To secure the grant for another year the Repetition must be more expressive and the intelligence with the meaning greater.

My Lords have ordered the grant for the class of infants to be reduced by one-tenth under Article 115 for defective teaching."

Attendance at school seems to have been a problem at this time. The average attendance dropped by twenty four children in the annual report. The day the Inspector called only thirteen children were present.

In September 1891, The Free Education Act was passed in Parliament and the Vicar, Rev. Algernon Ryder, wrote in the Parish Magazine: -

"Today the Free Education Act, as it is called, of 1891 comes into force and the parents in our parish will no longer have to supply their children with pence when they send them off to school on Monday mornings. There was a time, as older people will know, when there was very little education to be got in country parishes; then schools began to increase and grants of money were given by the government. Next came compulsory education and now, lastly, has come free education. It is well, at such a time, that those who have received education in village schools should remember that the pence they have carried to school have paid a very small share of the cost of their schooling and that they should feel grateful to those who have subscribed large amounts each year that they may have good teaching. Those who have found it a hard struggle to provide for their children will be thankful for the relief of not having to pay the school pence and those who could better afford the school pence will feel it a privilege to give what they can.

It is greatly to be hoped that in no case the parent's feeling of responsibility for their children will be lessened by their paying nothing towards their education or that because it costs them nothing they will value it less."

There were several severe epidemics the following year: scarlet fever, typhoid fever, measles, whooping cough and ringworm. The school was closed for one week in May in an attempt to stop the infections spreading. Some children were very ill and an absence from school of twelve or thirteen weeks with scarlet fever was quite common.

In 1885 the Inspector's report comments that "Spelling was very unsatisfactory, the mistakes being too numerous and the singing was too harsh."

Attendance at school increased during the next few years and in 1887 there were thirty five infants in a room which could accommodate only twenty one children under the official ruling of 8 square feet per child. The Managers were told by the Inspector that arrangements must be made to enlarge the premises or next year's grant might be withheld. The Managers acted promptly and a separate Infant Room, independent of the Junior School Room, was built. The Managers were congratulated by the Inspector the following year on the "bright and cheerful new Infant Room."

Further entries in the School Log were: -

**1888**

Mar. 5    Several children away this afternoon to see the opening of the new railway line at Hinton Station.

April    Classes worked on paper instead of slates.

In the June edition of the Parish Magazine the Vicar points out the serious financial difficulties of the school. He wrote: -

"It will be seen, on referring to the balance sheet of the School, that we begin the school year with a debt of £7 1s. 5d. The Managers finding the difficulty in raising the necessary funds to keep the school going and fearing an increase of the debt on the working of the present year, felt obliged to reduce the Master's salary by £20."

Later that year a further crisis occurred when Her Majesty's Inspector reported that one member of staff was quite inadequate for teaching 69 children. So the Rev. Filleul wrote in the Parish Magazine: -

"We are advertising for a Pupil Teacher to help in the School, according to the Government Inspector's Order, or a female assistant might suit equally well. Any person, though uncertificated, provided she can really be of some use in the teaching of the lower standards would satisfy the requirements of the code. We are offering £16 to £20 salary according to the capabilities of the teacher. Her work would be six hours a day attendance in the School for five days a week. Can any of our readers recommend anyone for the place?

It would be better to have someone from the neighbourhood who could live at home, since the salary is so small. Now that we have a railway station so near and convenient, morning and evening trains, it may be possible to engage someone from Bournemouth, Christchurch or other neighbouring town, where there must be many seeking employment, even some delicate person might be heard of, who would be glad to winter in the south of England and find the light work enough to undertake. We must engage an assistant as soon as possible."

Two years later the Vicar congratulated the staff: -

"Mr. Ellwood has now worked the School up to its best and Miss Vicary's work is specially commended. At the same time there can be no question that our blot is in the matter of School attendance. After making every allowance for sickness and those living a distance, there remains the fact that some of the parents are all too careless about their children's education, whilst others whose children are making the best possible averages, deserve the highest commendation; the latter will appreciate the new medals awarded for good attendance."

The Annual School Treat was enjoyed by all and reported in the Parish magazine: -

**August 1890**

"The annual treat to the children of the day and Sunday Schools took place on Thursday, July 31st. Tea was served to about 130 in the Schoolroom at half past three, after which they walked in procession to Beacon Lodge where various games were indulged in with much heartiness until darkness came on. The Marchioness of Waterford, Lady Jane Ellis, William Ellis, Esq., Captain and Mrs. Hone, E.H. Bellairs, Esq., and several others were present and gave prizes for racing, etc. Lady Waterford distributed medals to five boys and girls who had been most regular in their attendance at School."

The Diocesan Inspector visited the School regularly and examined the children in Catechism and in reciting passages from the Bible. The Vicar records the visit of one Inspector in December, 1890: -

"Among the events of the past month in our Parish the inspection of the School in religious subjects by the Diocesan Inspector is to be noted. His report is given below and it is the cause of gratitude to God that the young amongst us are being so well taught in the most important part of their education, and we must not forget to be grateful to those who teach them so carefully day by day. The report says, 'The infant room passed an exceptionally good examination, answering being unusually bright, correct and general. There has also been very good work in the other parts of the School and the Senior division in particular showed as a rule accurate and intelligent knowledge. But both in this and in Division 2 there were a few children who seemed to know little or nothing, owing to the fact that having to come from a long distance they do not get to school in time for the religious instruction. This is more to be regretted because the children who give themselves a chance of being taught are evidently taught very well indeed. The written exercises were satisfactory and the tone and discipline were good.'
Signed: T. Lewis Davis, Diocesan Inspector"

At the beginning of the 19th century there was practically no secondary education apart from the few public schools and the old endowed Grammar schools in this country. It was impossible for an ordinary working class lad to continue his education after the age of 13. But the residents of Highcliffe were indeed fortunate. In 1869 an evening school for boys only, between the ages 13 years and 21 years, was started by the schoolmaster. It was open on Monday, Wednesday and Thursday evenings for not less than two hours at a time and the fee was 2d. a week. The records show that the Evening Continuation School was attended regularly.

Some years later, in 1891, the Government put a large amount of money at the disposal of the County Council for technical education. Classes were to be held at larger centres, like Christchurch, in applied mechanics, cookery, mechanical drawing and carpentry. Highcliffe, too, was to be part of this plan. The classes were advertised in the Parish Magazine: -

"In October, on four of the Saturday evenings, a lecturer is to come to the Highcliffe School to lecture on agricultural engineering. Though this sounds a difficult subject it will include all kinds of practical, useful and interesting subjects such as the measuring of gravel, of timber, of wells, of land and other things of quite a different kind such as drainage and sanitary matters."

The four lectures were such a success and so well attended that it was decided to continue the instruction on a regular basis and General Stuart of Hoburne generously offered to pay the costs, so that there would be no charge for attendance.

The Vicar reports the progress of the Night School: -

"It is very satisfactory to see how the men and boys have been glad to avail themselves of the opportunities of improving themselves in these cold winter evenings. The night school has been very well attended. If others want to come, let them do so at once. Monday, Tuesday and Friday are the nights at 7.00 p.m. The Ambulance classes on Thursdays at the Jubilee Room (now Highcliffe Sports and Social Club) at 8.00 are full of interest and usefulness and are much appreciated. The series of lectures on horticulture every Wednesday at 7.00 in the School may show us how to make our gardens more productive and so are likely to be popular."

In August 1892 the Annual School Treat was held at Beacon Lodge. An account of the festivities appears in the Parish Magazine: -

"On Wednesday the children of the Highcliffe Day and Sunday School held their annual treat in Beacon Lodge Park, kindly lent for the occasion by Mr. Nugent. The scholars of late have been rapidly increasing and now number about 170. All thoroughly enjoyed themselves excepting one little boy, W. Derham, who in jumping, fell and dislocated his elbow. Immediately upon the accident, the little fellow was conveyed to Dr. Hartford's surgery at Christchurch, accompanied by Dr. Culling, a visitor to Beacon Lodge and Mr. Skinner, and he is now going on very favourably."

# Chapter Eight

# THE SCHOOLS

At the end of the 1890's there was no dramatic event to mark the beginning of a new century. Fighting continued in South Africa in the Boer War, costing the country £222 million and was to continue for a further two years. News reached Highcliffe of a milestone in that war. The School Record reads: -

**March 1st 1900**

"News received today of the relief of Ladysmith. The children therefore at 12 noon, in the presence of the Vicar, sang *Rule Britannia* and the National Anthem, gave three hearty cheers for General Buller and his brave soldiers."

School attendance was still a problem. At the Petty Sessions, Thomas Rickman of Highcliffe was summoned for not sending his children to school and was fined five shillings. William Broom, too, was similarly fined, his daughter having made only three out of thirty attendances and her sister seventeen out of thirty attendances.

The Evening Continuation School continued to be well attended and the curriculum was increased to include Commercial Arithmetic, Geography and Drawing.

In 1902 Mr. A.J. Balfour, the Prime Minister, passed a further Education Act through Parliament which gave the sole power for primary and secondary education to the County Councils. This system continues today.

A very distinguished guest staying at the Castle in 1907 was the German Emperor – the Kaiser. He was particularly fond of children and had planned a special treat for the children of Highcliffe village. It was to be an outing to the New Forest but, unfortunately, the weather was unsuitable. The Kaiser suggested a tea party in the schoolroom. The occasion was supposed to be quite informal. The Kaiser had wished it to be "just the children and myself," but the crowds came to Highcliffe in the hope of seeing the Kaiser. One newspaper report estimated that there were a thousand people outside the school. The event was recorded in the national and local press and the Parish Magazine: -

**January 1908 – The German Emperor's Tea**

"No greater honour has been done to the school-children in our Parish than the tea so kindly given by the German Emperor on St. Andrew's Day, coupled with the welcome presence of his Majesty in person. For several days previously, the village street had been afflair with buntings, the British and German flags hanging side by side. On the eventful day the schoolroom was decorated, the tables laid out with choice cakes and bread and butter. A special portion at the entrance to the room was carpeted with red felt on which was placed a tea table and a bank of flowers behind. This was reserved for the Emperor and his suite. At 5.15p.m. His Majesty arrived and found the children already seated at tea, according to his expressed and thoughtful desire. He was received by the Vicar and his daughter and Miss Cameron who were presented to him and with whom he remained talking for some time. Both the Emperor and his suite were much pleased with the scene. The Emperor expressed himself to be delighted with the way the children were dressed and the way they did their hair.

He graciously accepted two baskets of flowers which were gracefully offered to him by two little girls. After two flashlight photographs had been taken, His Majesty walked down the room amongst the children and teachers and cut the cake, standing six feet high, which he had sent over especially from the Castle.

On leaving the children rose and cheered the Emperor most heartedly, the cheers being taken up by the crowd of people who stood outside. The occasion showed not merely the Emperor's well known love of children, but a Royal graciousness which won all hearts."

Mr. Horatio Ellwood had been the headmaster of the School for forty years from 1882 to 1922. He had lived at the schoolhouse, where his first daughter was born, and later at Moorfields, the house that was part of the Stuart Trust on the school site. Some time later he built several houses in Lymington Road and lived in one, 'Holmlea'. His whole life was devoted to the school and his pupils. The last Inspector's Report the school received under the headship of Mr. Ellwood included the following: -

"The head teacher will retire at the end of this term after more than forty years continuous service in the school. He has fully earned the gratitude of the managers and the Local Education Authority. His pride and interest in his work show no sign of diminishing with advancing years."

Mr. Ellwood himself wrote in the School Log: -

"**December 22nd 1922**. School closed this afternoon for the usual two weeks holiday. Before leaving, as I do with a broken heart, I wish to place on record my gratitude to my staff. – *H. Ellwood*"

On his retirement Mr. Ellwood was presented with a blue leather memorial in which were written the names of the managers of the school, the teachers and the pupils at that time. The book, decorated in gold leaf, was kept by his daughter, Miss M. Ellwood, who was a district nurse in the village and lived in Highcliffe.

The new head teacher was Mr. W. Newby Stubbs. He has been described as a 'giant of a man'. He continued recording events at the school: -

**1933**

June        School closed for the day for the Methodist Sunday School outing.

**1934**

Oct.21      Magic lantern show given by the headmaster, with the assistance of
            Mr. Toms who provided electrical current from the engine in the
            school house.

**1935**

May 24      Hon. Mrs. Stuart Wortley called and presented each child with a copy
            of the King's broadcast speech.

**1937**

Nov. 8      Free milk scheme started for all children of school age.

ST. MARK'S CHURCH SCHOOL, HIGHCLIFFE

The old village life was to change quite dramatically during the winter of
1939. Hitler had invaded Poland and on September 3rd 1939, Neville Chamberlain
declared war on Germany. Fathers and elder brothers were 'called up' to serve
their country in one of the armed forces, leaving mothers and sisters at home on

81

their own. Children were evacuated from the large cities and towns such as Southampton and Portsmouth to the safer areas in the country. Children came from those cities to spend the war years in Highcliffe.

Trenches were dug in the woods adjacent to the school playground to ensure the safety of the children during air raids. There was no direct attack on Highcliffe itself. The only bombs dropped were those on the return flight of the enemy planes, to empty their bomb-loads before flying back over the Channel and landing.

This, of course, was not known at the time so that when the air raid siren sounded the children left their classrooms and filed into the trenches where they sometimes had to spend as long as three hours. They were kept amused by their teachers with singing and in competitions and puzzles. When the 'All Clear' sounded they returned to their lessons in the school.

The Second World War years were recorded in the School Log: -

## 1939

September    School remained closed for an entire week because of the state of emergency. School re-opened as a Junior School, all the senior pupils had transferred to Ashley Secondary School. The school would work a double shift system sharing the school with the Southampton children.

Oct. 6    Air Raid Wardens called to ensure all gas masks fitted.

## 1940

Jan. 8    School re-opened at 12.45. Southampton evacuees having had the morning session. Football Club gave permission for matches to be played on the Recreation Ground. They would not allow practise games on their pitch and were unable to lend footballs to the school.

Feb. 19    School merged with the Evacuee Dept. and began to work full-time, there being 27 Southampton and private evacuees.

July 3    Air raid siren sounded – children went to trenches – raiders passed over – all clear in half an hour.

Aug. 28    Bombs were dropped in the neighbourhood.

Sept. 10    Village had disturbed night – bombs dropped.

Sirens sounded practically every day, July, August, September, December. Planes passed over.

## 1941

Feb. 4    First treatment of diphtheria was given to 47 children by Dr. Parker-Williams.

Trenches became too damp so children remained at school when the sirens sounded.

| May 12 | 21 Portsmouth evacuees admitted. |

**1942**

| Dec. 14 | Emergency kitchen started in playground. |

**1943**

| May 7 | A bomb fell in the woods near the school and the blast caused damage to the windows and panes and ceilings. |

**1944**

| May 15 | An American Thunderbolt aeroplane, which had been on a raid over France, returned with a damaged undercarriage. The plane could not land safely on the Christchurch Airfield because of the bomb store there. It attempted to land on the Recreation Ground at Highcliffe but missed and landed on the school playground. |

In 1945 the school was fitted with electricity and two dances were held in the Parish Hall to raise the money to purchase a master wireless with loudspeakers in each classroom. These were later installed.

There were now no difficulties with attendance. In 1947 there was not sufficient room to accommodate all the children and the Infant class of forty children used the Parish Hall in Gordon Road.

To celebrate the Coronation of Queen Elizabeth II in 1953 the Mayor and Mayoress of Christchurch, with the Mace Bearer, visited the school and presented each child with a Coronation Mug provided by the Corporation. In addition further gifts of a New Testament and a Coronation shilling were given to each child to mark the historic day.

It was about this time that the village of Highcliffe began to change. The old country village image was to disappear with the breaking up of the large estates for housing. St. Mark's School became very overcrowded and it looked as though the days of the village school were numbered too. In the Parish Magazine, dated July 1958, Rev. R. Barnett wrote: -

**New School for Highcliffe – Ministry Approval**

"The School Managers have been informed that the Minister of Education has now decided upon the major building programme for Hampshire for 1959-60. A new two-form entry Junior School at Highcliffe has been included in that programme. The School is to be built on a part of the Wolhayes Estate, adjacent to Chewton Common. At present the site is somewhat inaccessible, but it is understood that planning permission has been given to those developing the Wolhayes and Holmhurst Estates for new roads, more or less linking Pinewood Close and Wharncliffe Road and Chewton Common Road and Hinton Wood Avenue. These new roads, with others in the same area, will result in the School being a fairly easy walk from most parts of the Parish. It is understood that the Education Authority proposes that the new School shall be a Junior School and will accommodate 320 pupils."

Mr. R. Chacksfield was chosen from more than two hundred applicants for the post of Headmaster to the new school. Work on the school had just begun so Mr. Chacksfield became Headmaster of St. Mark's Church of England Junior and Infant School at Easter 1960 when Miss Quelch retired. The older children would later become the nucleus of the new Highcliffe Junior School and the younger children would remain and a separate headteacher would be appointed for St. Mark's Infant School.

The Parish Magazine records the changing scene in the educational life of the village: -

### October 1961

"An outward visible sign of the educational changes in this district is the change in the School uniform now being worn by many of our children. The very smart dark green blazer with silver piping, the cap and beret and tie to match is the uniform of the new Highcliffe County Primary School. The uniform was originally ordered by Mr. Chacksfield in the expectation that by now his new school would have been opened. A slight link with St. Mark's, the parent school, remains in the lion emblazoned as a badge on the pocket. Unfortunately, the lion has lost his wings and has become simple, though very elegant lion rampant, with no apparent local connection. The badge of St. Mark's School remains as before, the winged lion, traditional emblem of our patron saint. The other new school uniform to be seen locally is that of Christchurch Grammar School, temporarily sharing accommodation with the new Gore Secondary School in Milton. In two year's time when the building, near Hoburne, is completed, the Grammar School will move there. This uniform is a deep purple in colour bearing on the blazer pocket a badge showing a forest tree with the waves symbolic of its situation of the school 'twixt sea and forest'."

The new Junior School building was ready for the beginning of the new school year, September 1962. Children over the age of seven were transferred to the new building while the younger children remained in the old building under the headship of Mrs. Harrison.

The building of the new Junior School had started in December 1959 and was completed by May 1962 at a cost of £59,000. The official opening of the school was recorded for the Parish Magazine: -

**April 1963**

"A very happy ceremony took place when Mr. J.H. Cordle, our Member of Parliament, formally opened Highcliffe County Junior School, almost a year after the building had been taken into use. This delay had given time for the various teething troubles to be overcome and for the grounds to be properly laid out. In his speech the Member reminded his very distinguished audience of the three essential influences on each child – the family, the school and the church. All were essential for the proper development of the child. Later in the proceedings, after prayers by the Methodist Minister, the School was dedicated by the Vicar."

Some items from the School Log indicate the development of the schools in Highcliffe: -

| | | |
|---|---|---|
| 1962 | Sept. 28th | A meeting of teachers, parents and friends at the Junior School took the decision to build a swimming pool in the school grounds. |
| 1963 | May 14th | Excavations for the swimming pool were begun by the Military Engineering Experimental Establishments by kind permission of Brig. Jarrett Kerr. |
| 1964 | March 8th | Opening of Christchurch Grammar School (now Highcliffe School). |
| | June 27th | The Junior School swimming pool was officially opened by Air Vice Marshal B.A. Chacksfield, who arrived by helicopter. |
| | Sept. 8th | The changing rooms and the fencing round the Junior School swimming pool were given by Christchurch Grammar School. |
| 1967 | April 5th | The little school at Hinton closed and the ten children were transferred to the Highcliffe Junior School. |
| | May 22nd | Mr. Chacksfield talked to the parents on the Plowden Report. |
| 1968 | March 29th | Building of the new Infant School began on land adjacent to the Junior School |
| 1970 | June 17th | The official opening of the new Infant School by the Bishop of Southampton. The old school, known now as The Annexe, continued to be used by the Infant School. |
| 1973 | July 5th | The Junior School Choir, trained by Miss Denniss, entered the Llangollen International Music Festival for the first time. |
| 1974 | April 1st | All schools were transferred from the Hampshire County Education Dept. to the Dorset County Education Dept. |
| 1975 | Oct. 24th | The great elm on the playing fields at the Junior School had to be felled. |

## Private Schools in Highcliffe

There were three private schools in Highcliffe. The largest was St. George's School, an Anglican girl's day and boarding school. The House was originally Shelley Hill, the home of Edward Huntly Hooper; it stood well back from the road between St. Georges Close and Curzon Way. The extensive grounds included woods, swimming pool, playing fields and tennis courts. The principals were Miss Harwood and Miss Norman. The uniform was Wedgwood blue blazers. When the school closed the Vicar wrote in the Parish Magazine: -

## April 1961

"There will be much regret locally at the news that St. George's School is to close down at the end of the forthcoming summer term. For many years past, under the headship of Miss M.G. Harwood and her late partner, Miss E. Norman, this school has given an excellent general education to a large number of children of this parish and neighbourhood. There are two reasons why we are sorry that the school is closing: firstly and chiefly because there will no longer be an Anglican Private School in the parish and secondly because we shall very much miss the presence of the boarders at the service of the church."

Another was Luckhams School which used Cranemoor House. It was a prep school for young gentlemen. The third school was Waterford House, a small school for boys. They wore pink caps with 'W.H.' embroidered on them.

# Chapter Nine

# THE VILLAGE IN THE NINETEENTH CENTURY

Few written records exist which cast light on life in Newtown during the first part of the 19th century; however, the *Christchurch Times* was established in 1855 and the Parish Magazine commenced publication in 1888. From these two sources it is possible to trace the events which took place in the village during that period.

The following extracts provide a commentary on the development of the village: -

**January 20th 1866**

"The bridge called Humphrey's Bridge on the road from Lymington to Christchurch has been destroyed by the flood occasioned by the fall of snow and the thaw which succeeded it, which swelled the little brook until it became a torrent."

**January 1868**

"It being the wish of several inhabitants of Newtown and its neighbourhood to establish a Reading Room. A suitable room was offered by Mr. Frampton, Grocer and it was unanimously resolved to form a society, 25 persons gave their names as members."

The Mudeford Sandbank extended along the coast beyond Highcliffe Castle creating a 'run' between it and the cliffs which sometimes froze in winter making a natural rink for skaters. The sand bar also provided a hazard for shipping.

**May 1875**

"Immediate sale of the hull of the ketch *Eliza* driven ashore on the Christchurch bar, opposite Highcliffe Castle, which Messrs. Abbott & Sons are instructed by Mr. Lawrence to sell by auction at the above spot on Saturday next, May 15th, 1875 at 3 o'clock.

It appears she was in the roads when she parted her cable, came broadside on the bar, and was immediately rendered helpless. The cargo of coal has since been got out of her hold."

**1882**

"Lady Waterford established a milk shop – a Temperance Lodge – in the village to encourage the inhabitants to drink milk instead of spirits. She painted the shop sign herself, a brown cow on an olive green grass background."

One of the rooms in the school was used by the Temperance Society but Lady Waterford, a strict teetotaller herself, decided to commemorate Queen Victoria's Jubilee by presenting the village with its own Reading Room which was to be built on the site now occupied by Highcliffe Sports and Social Club.

## October 30th 1886

"On Thursday evening in connection with the Temperance Society a very pleasant entertainment was given in the schoolroom by the children of the Band of Hope, a service of song rendered, entitled 'For Harry's Sake', the connective parts being read by the Marchioness of Waterford."

Plans for the Jubilee Reading Room were beginning to take shape. In one of her letters reproduced in the book *Two Noble Lives*, by Augustus Hare, Lady Waterford writes: -

## July 11th 1887

"Mr. Bellairs, the Highcliffe Agent, is now in full swing of help to me about the Reading Room here which I mean to begin as soon as possible. I have also to increase the Infant School by throwing in the old Reading room, so it becomes imperative to do the new one, but I am determined not to ask from a soul for it and with the two contributions of £50 I have enough without …"

## July 1887

"The celebration of the Jubilee was arranged at Highcliffe by a committee consisting of Gen. and Mrs. Stuart, Capt. Ogle and Messrs. Pack, Proudly and Ellwood and took place on Friday, June 24th when the parishioners were entertained at a most substantial meat tea which had been defrayed by subscriptions collected by the committee. Early in the morning, the members of the committee … erected a tent in the field opposite the Vicarage (which was kindly lent for the occasion by Lady Waterford) and by the addition of flags lent by the officers of the coastguards at Barton and Mudeford, the field presented a very gay and festive appearance … At the Castle gate was erected a beautiful arch of evergreens, bearing the words, 'God save the Queen' in large letters. Upon arriving at the grounds, tea had been provided by the Marchioness of Waterford in The Avenue, whither the children proceeded. At half past four nearly 320 parishioners sat down to a substantial meat tea, the fare comprising bread, ham, mutton and shrimps … after tea Lady Waterford kindly threw open the Castle grounds … Races and swings were arranged and dancing was enjoyed to the strains of the band. A pleasant holiday was brought to an end by a display of fireworks (given by Mrs. Stuart) on the beach."

FRAMPTON'S IN LYMINGTON ROAD
(He had a passion for windmills)

**November 5th 1887**

"On Tuesday the new hall and Jubilee Reading Room at Highcliffe was opened by the Marchioness of Waterford. This hall which is built at the far end of the village of Newtown was erected by funds provided by Lady Waterford and a few of her friends. It measures 60 ft. by 20 ft. and is intended for a working men's reading room and a hall for lectures, entertainments, etc. It is built of brick, the walls inside being cemented and it has a board ceiling, the roof being covered with felt and corrugated iron, and will be heated by means of open fire places. The building is ornamented with terra cotta mullioned windows and doorway by Messrs. Jennings of Parkstone and over the north window is a very beautifully executed medallion of the Queen by Messrs. Doulton of Lambeth. On the outside wall, facing the main road, is the inscription '1887 Jubilee Reading Room'. The ceremony commenced by the formal unveiling of the Queen by Lady Waterford ... and Mr. Bellairs expressed the great pleasure he had had in designing, with Lady Waterford's assistance, the hall in which they were met ... the presence of Mrs. Maberly reminded him ... that that lady had built from his plans a room for the people of Mudeford and Stanpit ... He was glad to feel that no contracting builder had been employed. The brickwork had been carried out by Mr. Thomas Tiller in a most satisfactory manner and the carpenter's work by Mr. George Forward ... The Rev. Filleul reminded them of the next great work in hand, which was the church roof … and the president, Lady Waterford, having declared the room open, members were enrolled …"

## May 1888

"It may be useful to teetotallers amongst us to know that Framptons at the P.O. sell ingredients for making a nice temperance drink, bitter and wholesome. This drink improves greatly by being kept in a bottle for a few weeks.

Some may be glad to hear of a really good filter for water. Many filters are worse than useless but this is strongly recommended by doctors and has won medals at exhibitions. The makers of it are Cheavins of Boston."

## January 1890

"It should be recorded that Lady Waterford has added to the money already given, showing her interest in the good of the parish, in the building of a house for an attendant to the Jubilee Room. Its first occupant Mr. Baker, is now established there with his wife and family, he has just retired from the Royal Navy after 29 years of service."

## March 1891

"You will find below the accounts of the Relief Work. Though they were on a small scale yet were a help to some who were willing to work, but had no employment at the time. Thanks are due to those who contributed to the Fund and several of those who benefited by the work expressed their thanks to me, so that I may assure those who helped that there was gratitude felt for the kindness shown. And this kindness was far from being only in the way of money gifts. General Stuart (Hoburne) most kindly allowed gravel to be taken from his gravel pit. Mr. James Proudly was most kind in giving much time and trouble and superintending the mending or making of the path to Gus. Moreover, he and Sir John Thursby (Holmhurst) gave the use of their horses and carts. Messrs. Frampton and Sons lent barrows. Barrows were also lent from the Highcliffe Gardens through Mr. Skinner. And in the laying out of the small remainder of the fund lately in improving the path and a road across Chewton Common, Mr. Frederick Frampton has taken the superintendancy and given help in other ways. Though the Works have been small works we may be thankful that the men were able to earn money when the pinch was being most felt at the end of a long frost, and that as a result of this work, people will be able to go to Church or elsewhere with drier feet, and children will be not so be likely to catch cold, through sitting in schools with damp shoes in wet weather."

# RELIEF WORKS FUND

| RECEIPTS | £ | s. | d. | EXPENDITURE | £ | s. | d. |
|---|---|---|---|---|---|---|---|
| Sir John Thursby, Bart | 1 | 0 | 0 | 109 day's Work divided among | | | |
| Lady Amphlett | 1 | 0 | 0 | 17 Men at 2s. a day | 10 | 18 | 0 |
| Mrs. Entwistle | 1 | 16 | 0 | Hire of Carts | 1 | 19 | 6 |
| Miss Martin | 1 | 0 | 0 | Sharpening Tools | 0 | 4 | 0 |
| Mrs. Braddyll | 1 | 10 | 0 | | | | |
| Captain Holme | 0 | 10 | 0 | | | | |
| Rev. Algernon C.D. Ryder | 2 | 10 | 0 | | | | |
| Mrs. Algernon Ryder | 2 | 10 | 0 | | | | |
| Surveyor of Highways | 0 | 10 | 0 | | | | |
| Frampton & Sons (Builders) | 0 | 10 | 0 | | | | |
| Mr Frampton (Grocer) | 0 | 2 | 0 | | | | |
| Mr. Ford | 0 | 2 | 6 | | | | |
| Mr. Lawrence | 0 | 1 | 0 | | | | |
| | £13 | 1 | 6 | | £13 | 1 | 6 |

The National Fire Service was not to come into being for another fifty years, but the village had its own Fire Brigade and all its members were volunteers.

The following is a copy of the Captain's report of the fire in Millhams Street, Christchurch: -

## October 1891

"September 29th – Called to a fire at Christchurch. Call given by C. Peckham, postman, at 7.25 p.m. Called out six men and got engine horsed. Arrived with engine and six men at 8.15 p.m. Other men following immediately. Found three cottages in Millhams Street one sheet of flame. Christchurch Brigade already at work but not able to do much owing to bursted hose, etc. Got men to work on left wing and after some difficulty got fire under. Captain Langley, with detachment of soldiers, rendered great assistance. Left fire about 12.45 a.m. Three cottages completely burnt out but fire prevented from spreading. Cause of fire attributed to a chimney catching but nothing known for certain. Men behaved splendidly, had great difficulty in starting, through lamps burning badly, engine worked well and hose in good order.

FRANCIS P. LATHAM, Captain
Highcliffe Volunteer Fire Brigade"

In August 1892, Major and Mrs. Stuart Wortley allowed parishioners to stroll in the gardens of the Castle on Sundays to enjoy the beautiful flowers, shrubs and trees. The majority of parishioners enjoyed this privilege but there were some that took advantage of the invitation.

"By Major Stuart Wortley's kindness the grounds and gardens of Highcliffe Castle will be open again to Parishioners on Sunday November the 13th and on following Sundays until further notice. Owing to the mis-use of the privilege by some boys, whom Major Stuart Wortley found stealing fruit, he has been obliged to dis-allow the entrance of boys under 18 in future."

Note in the above report by the Captain of the Volunteer Fire Brigade the general change of name for the village – Slop Pond, Newtown and now Highcliffe.

MAIN STREET HIGHCLIFFE

### December 1892 – Highcliffe Post Office

"The following letter from the Secretary at the General Post Office is the final and satisfactory answer to the memorial signed by many Parishioners which represented that as there were some twenty other Newtowns in England and Wales and as four of these were in Hampshire, it would be a great advantage to save letters and telegrams from mis-carrying by changing the name of our Post Office to Highcliffe.

'Sir, in reply to the memorial recently received signed by yourself and other residents in the neighbourhood of Highcliffe, I am directed by the Post Master General to inform you that under the circumstances of the case it was decided that the designation of the Post Office at Newtown, Christchurch, be changed from Newtown to Highcliffe in accordance with the wishes of the memorialists. I am, Sir, Your Obedient Servant, Edward Yield.'

Now that the name of the Post Office is changed it is not impossible that the name Newtown may gradually be dropped altogether."

SHOPS IN LYMINGTON ROAD
OPPOSITE POST OFFICE

### The Spelling of the word Highcliffe

"A valued correspondent raises a point in regard to the spelling of Highcliffe without an 'e'. The latter part of the word 'cliff' is, of course, derived from the verb to cleave. Formerly spelt Cleft, Clift, Cliffe, as well as Cliff. In old proper names in which it was compounded, the terminal 'e' seems to have been retained, we have examples of Cliffe in Wharncliffe Woods and Shorncliffe Camp. Old documents are extant with Highcliffe spelt with an 'e' as well as without."

# Chapter Ten

# THE VILLAGE IN THE TWENTIETH CENTURY

THE VILLAGE, HIGH CLIFFE

The beginning of this century heralded more changes than any previous century. Cars and aeroplanes were to revolutionise travel; radio and television would broaden people's outlook. The British Empire was to disappear gradually and there were to be two world wars, but in Highcliffe at the beginning of the century, life was still centred in the village. Occasionally there was the opportunity to travel to neighbouring towns as the following advertisement shows: -

**January 1900**

"JOHN SAUNDERS, Highcliffe, is running a light Spring covered van between Highcliffe and Lymington every Tuesday and Saturday, leaving Highcliffe at 8.30 a.m. and returning at 4 o'clock.

Also between Highcliffe and Christchurch on Wednesdays, leaving Highcliffe at noon, returning from the Wagon and Horses, Christchurch at 2 o'clock."

A month later in the Parish Magazine there was further good news for the inhabitants of Highcliffe: -

## February 17th 1900

"The supply of water to Highcliffe is now completed, the water being let into the mains on Wednesday last."

In 1901, the Board of Agriculture figures show that the Parish of Highcliffe consisted of 2,615 acres of which: -

| | |
|---|---|
| 120 | acres were covered by the tide |
| 4 | acres by inland waterway |
| 141 | acres of foreshore |
| 896¾ | acres of arable land |
| 539¼ | acres of permanent grass |
| 154 | acres of woods and plantations |

The remaining 760 acres were presumably houses, shops and churches.

There has been mention in previous chapters of the building of the Parish Hall in 1906, the visit of the Kaiser in 1907 and the building of the Primitive Methodist Chapel in 1908. That year too, the image of the Jubilee Reading Room changed. On November 7th, Brig. Gen. Edward Stuart Wortley re-opened the Room as licensed premises.

There were no banking facilities in Highcliffe at this time. Three times a week a clerk from Lloyds Bank in Christchurch took the train to Hinton Admiral Station where he was met by Harry Lee in Reek's, the butcher, cart. He was taken to Reek's shop (later the International Store, now Somerfields) where he used the side room for banking transactions. Lloyds was the first bank in Highcliffe, the present building being completed in 1912.

The nearest doctor at this time was Dr. Hartford who lived at the Square House in Christchurch. Dr. Brooks recalls the story told him by Mrs. Rogers of how she had to walk to Christchurch to collect medicines from Dr. Hartford's housekeeper, who would light a candle for her return trip. The road then was a small country lane which was narrow and dark because of the tall trees growing from the banks on either side of the lane. On one such occasion she was frightened by a light coming in the opposite direction, whereupon she hid in the ditch. She watched, alarmed, as the light coming towards her wobbled and fell into the same ditch. It was her mother who had come to look for her.

There were no Parish Magazines for the years 1909-1919 and therefore a reliable source of information about those years is missing. Reference has previously been made to the building of Greystones by Captain and Mrs. Denison in 1913. At this time there was serious flooding at Sea Corner. The drains were unable to cope with heavy falls of rain and at one point a boat had been used to carry out rescue operations.

It was during the same year that Gen. Edward Stuart Wortley invited a Mr. Green to lay out a nine-hole golf course on the Castle estate. The site chosen was an area of about 40 acres west of the Castle and fronting on the Lymington Road. It was opened by the Princess Christian and the Princess Victoria. Mr. Percival became the next professional followed by Mr. Cecil Sergeant. The Club expanded rapidly and in 1927 the course was extended to 18 holes and in recognition of Mr. Sergeant's care and devotion to the Golf Club, the Nineteenth Hole was christened 'Cecil's Bar'.

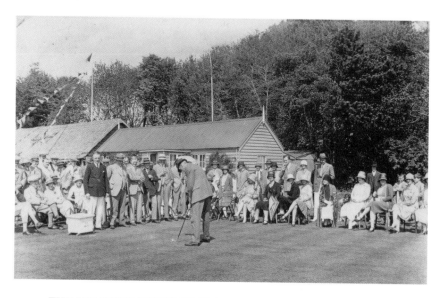

THE INAUGURATION OF HIGHCLIFFE GOLF COURSE 1927
The President Maj.Gen. Hon. Edward Stuart Wortley drives off with a silver putter
Club Captain Maj. P.A. Brooke standing behind the tee box.

In 1949, before the Castle was sold outside the Stuart family, the Golf Club members purchased the course from the Castle estate. A public footpath crosses the Golf Course from the Lymington Road to Avon Beach, allowing non-golfers a view of the beautifully kept greens.

On August 4th 1914, hostilities broke out in Europe with the invasion of Belgium by the Germans. The Great War had begun. It was to be a war unlike any previous war – men fought from trenches. Tanks were used for the first time and the Germans developed the great powered balloons called Zeppelins to bomb London.

The emancipation of women became a reality as they took the jobs of the men away serving their country in Europe. Britain had lost nearly 750,000 men, thirty-six from Highcliffe, before the cease-fire at 11 a.m. on November 11th 1918 – Armistice Day. On October 17th 1920 the Highcliffe War Memorial which stands at the junction of The Avenue and Hinton Wood Avenue, was unveiled and dedicated. The period between the Great War and the Second World War saw little change in the structure of the village.

In 1920 the *Grampus*, a coastal tug, was driven ashore at Highcliffe. The boiler can still be seen in the sea at low tide below the Cliff Car Park. The way down to the beach from Sea Corner was thickly wooded, with pine trees on either side of the path.

Highcliffe Corner was occupied by the blacksmiths, Walter and Harry Shave. The blacksmith stood outside the forge in his leather apron, beside a pile of horse-shoes, awaiting custom. Across the road, down to the sea, was a five-barred gate, a gap at the side allowing pedestrians to pass unhindered. There was another gate at the other end of Wharncliffe Road, near the Recreation Ground. Further down Waterford Road, on the left, stood Stuart Lodge, the Villa Matilda, extended in 1927 to become the Highcliffe Hotel, and Greystones. On the right was Newtown House, Waterford House and Windwhistle.

HIGHCLIFFE HOTEL

The tariff of the Highcliffe Hotel at that time makes interesting reading today:

*Terms include Bedroom, Light, Attendance, Boot cleaning,*
*Breakfast, Luncheon, Afternoon Tea and Dinner.*
*Each person from 4 1/2 guineas per week or 14/6 a day.*
*A La Carte*
*Breakfast 3/-        Luncheon 3/6*
*Tea 1/6            Dinner 5/-*
*Orchestra during the season and all holidays.*

TEA HOUSE c. 1926

A large wooden Tea House stood on the edge of the cliffs near where the shelter is now. The beach had lovely golden sands and was similar to the Bournemouth Beach today. John Frampton erected the first beach hut on the cliffs; found it a profitable concern and added further huts during the ensuing years. In the 1950's, Lou Strickland, a well-known worker on the cliffs, counted 101 huts arranged in three terraces. The cliffs were under the control of the Council from the 1930's.

In the thirties a hall was built in Lymington Road as an entertainment centre for the village. The Enterprise Hall catered for a variety of leisure time pursuits. Mrs. Winduss, who grew up in the village, remembers the fun fair on the flat roof with automatic games machines and a roller skating rink. The Hall below was used as a cinema and for dances. Dancing was to either Jay Elms and his band or Zoot Money and his Big Rock Band. After World War II the Hall was bought by the British Legion as their local headquarters. Recently the Hall was demolished and Homecliffe House, a block of flats, was built.

Mr. Lybert Durrant who moved to Highcliffe at the beginning of the twentieth century when he was eight years old remembered the way in which General Stuart Wortley and his wife looked after the village and its people. He recalls seeing a man drop a piece of paper in Waterford Road. General Stuart Wortley, walking with his dog, called out to him, "Pick that paper up, man." The man obediently picked up the offending piece of paper.

HIGHCLIFFE AMATUER DRAMATIC SOCIETY
PRESENTS DAVID GARRICK 1927
Standing left to right: Hon. Gertrude Napier, Major Percy Brooke,
Mr. Geoffrey Saye, Rev. Hatton, Mr. George Stone, Mrs Elsie Brooke,
Mr. Arthur Lawrie, Rev. Moore.
Front row: Miss Joyce Curzon Howe, Miss Dorothy Clutterbuck, Mrs. Watts

Mr. Durrant's uncle had worked on the cliffs all his life and was concerned about the erosion there. As he travelled to work each day he pulled up any weeds growing by the roadside and replanted them on the cliffs as a small contribution to stabilizing the cliffs. Towards the end of his life when he became ill, General Stuart Wortley visited him regularly, sometimes bringing a gift of food from the Castle or sometimes leaving a pound note.

The land at the junction of the Lymington Road and Wharncliffe Road was originally leased from General Stuart Wortley as a Recreation Ground for the village but in 1932 the Rural District of Christchurch bought the ground from the General for £1,750.

When war was declared in 1939 many local men left the security of the village to fight for their country. Those who were left behind were formed into local defence groups. The Home Guard, formerly the Local Defence Volunteers (L.D.V.), or as Mrs. Stuart Wortley called them, the 'Long Dentured Veterans', were kept busy. The Village had been divided up into one mile 'beats' which were patrolled by Air Raid Wardens with their Headquarters in the Parish Hall in Gordon Road.

Enemy aircraft were continually flying over Highcliffe to bomb the inland cities. Bombs were dropped near Lyme Crescent, on Cobb's Camp and on Chewton Common. The latter left a crater big enough to bury a double decker bus. Mrs. Stuart Wortley recalls that all the windows in the Castle were shattered, except those given by the Kaiser to commemorate his visit in 1907. A lone Italian fighter plane strafed the Castle with machine-gun fire leaving thirty bullet holes in the masonry.

Everyone in the village worked hard for the 'cause' – whether it was knitting comforts for the troops, making up food parcels or raising funds for a variety of needs.

Miss G. Rhymes and Miss A. Sque remember the Searchlight Battalion stationed on Edgar's Dairy's fields and the American soldiers who camped in Froggy Lane (the footpath from the Walkford Hotel to the Milestone).

On June 6th 1944 the villagers realized that something dramatic was about to happen. There was intense air activity and the surrounding roads were crowded with military vehicles and troops sitting waiting. The invasion of Normandy had begun.

After the war, Mrs. Stuart Wortley felt the inhabitants of Highcliffe should be officially thanked for their patriotic devotion during the war years. She invited to the Castle representatives of those who had shown the 'Highcliffe Spirit'. Her son-in-law, Lord Abingdon, officially thanked the people of Highcliffe for their efforts during the past six years. Amongst all the celebrations the twenty-four men and one nursing sister who died on active service were not forgotten.

Maps found at German Headquarters after the war revealed that the beaches around Christchurch Bay had been chosen as a landing place for a German invasion. The Highcliffe beach was totally inaccessible to the public. The cliffs were protected by mile upon mile of barbed wire and patrolled by members of the Home Guard. Concrete gun emplacements were mounted on the cliffs to deter any who dared approach the shore.

There was tremendous secrecy surrounding the part of the cliff top enclosed by a ten foot steel fence, inside which were a number of buildings. Rumour suggested that at least two hundred of the country's leading scientists were working there. It was not until after the war that it was known the secret work had been on radiolocation research and development.

Steamer Point was at one time the western part of Highcliffe Castle Estate with its hybrid rhododendrons and Holm oaks, an indication of ornamental planting. There is a footpath which climbs up towards the golf course it crosses an old sunken track which was the back drive to the Castle from the West Lodge at Humphrey's Bridge. This track was built with some purpose, with brick-lined cuttings to relieve the gradient. Its western part disappeared when Seaway Avenue was developed in the 1930's.

Steamer Point derived its name from the steamer which Lord Stuart de Rothesay beached and used as a sea-lodge until it became too damp. He then commissioned Bemister to build a cottage there and aptly named it 'Steamer Cottage'. Mr. H. Lee could recall a family called Purton who lived there. Mrs Purton walked to Highcliffe village every Friday to do her shopping, carrying a lantern for the return journey through the dark woods in the Castle grounds. Steamer Cottage was destroyed about fifty years ago by a violent storm.

RADOME AT STEAMER POINT

The western part of the Castle estate was bought by the Ministry of Defence. In 1939, when the Air Defence Research and Development Establishment (A.D.R.D.E.) set up at Somerford, Christchurch, there was a need for a cliff-top site to place aerials used with coastal defence radar; Steamer Point was chosen because of its clear seaward views and proximity to the Somerford site. But, in 1942, A.D.R.D.E. was moved hurriedly to Great Malvern, Worcestershire, as it was considered too vulnerable from enemy attack in the exposed position at Highcliffe.

A year later the war was swinging towards the build-up for the D-Day offensive and the need for improved Army communications systems saw the arrival at Somerford and Steamer Point of the Signals Research and Development

Establishment (S.R.D.E.), previously split between the sites of Woolwich and Horsham in Sussex. Steamer Point then began a particular association with research topics in telecommunications which had lasted for nearly thirty seven years. An early addition to the wartime staff were the members of the Polish Institute of Technical Research. This group were evacuated from their homeland when their country was invaded by the Germans. They had been working in London to perfect equipment for the Polish underground movement prior to their move to Highcliffe.

A familiar landmark which appeared at Steamer Point in the late 1960's was the large white plastic sphere (radome), housing equipment for communication by radio and orbiting satellites. Much appreciated as a navigational landmark by yachtsmen in Christchurch Bay, the radome, however, has disappeared, along with the S.R.D.E. from Steamer Point. The 1973 Defence White Paper announced that S.R.D.E. would be integrated with the Royal Radar Establishment at Malvern; by summer 1980 the withdrawal from Steamer Point was complete. The site was left vacant.

After the war a national housing shortage existed. There was a need for quickly available accommodation for families whose homes had been destroyed by enemy action or who were moving to new areas to work. In Highcliffe this need was met by the 'prefab village' which sprang up in 1946 at the end of Gordon Road. The life expectancy of an asbestos prefab was about ten years but many prefabs lasted thirty years and were demolished about 1975 when all the families were re-housed.

The period from 1950 saw tremendous changes in the appearance of the village. The large houses were left derelict or were demolished and the parkland associated with the houses was divided to make housing estates.

The process of turning Highcliffe from a rural community to an area of residential development was well under way by 1960. The well-designed bungalows in their idyllic setting, with the attractions of the sea and the Forest, drew people from all over the country to retirement at Highcliffe. With this influx of people from differing backgrounds the village changed from a close knit community to one of wider interests. People who had spent a lifetime in industry and commerce or who had lived and worked in one of the big cities all brought experiences to enrich the life of the village.

A growing indication of the importance of Highcliffe and the acknowledgement of the contribution its inhabitants could make to civil life was the election of Mrs. Wallis-Power to the office of Mayor of Christchurch. Her term of office was the years 1950-52 and she was the first Highcliffe resident to achieve the acclaim of her peers to become the first citizen of the Borough. Her dignity and charm, as well as her capacity for hard work, made her an ideal mayor. Mrs. Wallis-Power lived at Culmore in Wharncliffe Road but after the death of her husband, the estate was left to the children of his first marriage; she moved across the road to 'Braemar'.

Immediately afterwards another Highcliffe resident was awarded the same honour. Mr. Kenneth Ashcroft, who kept an off-licence shop in the village, was elected Mayor for the term 1952-53.

A resident's recollections of the village at that time are of interest. "Hens on the car park, which was Philps and Brown's, the corn and seed shop; a donkey looking over the fence in a field in Wortley Road (now the Methodist Church site); and a cow peeping over a gate in a field in Lymington Road (now Buce Hayes Close). A drapers shop (which stood opposite the Post Office) was owned by a quaint old lady. As one entered the shop a bell clanged, echoing through the shop. Some time would elapse before the sound of pattering feet and the rustle of silk heralded the arrival of the owner – an elderly lady dressed in a long black gown.

The village doctor at this time was Dr. Parker Williams, known affectionately by the residents as 'Parker Bill'. He was a gentleman and probably the last traditional 'family doctor' who regarded a daily visit essential if a child had measles but whose surgery (now Claire Court) was very cramped and without any modern facilities. He was joined by Dr. Carr and, later, by Dr. Falkner Lee."

Extracts from the Parish Magazines of this period reflect the many facets of the life of the village: -

### The Coronation – Celebrations in Highcliffe                    February 1953

"'God Save the Queen' will be spelt in letters of fire on the cliff top at Highcliffe on Coronation Day, the Village Coronation Committee reports. They have ordered a magnificent display of fireworks to conclude the celebrations. The Church is likely to be floodlit and a great bonfire on the cliffs will link with other celebration bonfires on the Isle of Wight and in Dorset and all over Britain. There will be a torchlight procession beginning at 9.30 p.m. at the cliff top. Dancing in both halls in the village will follow to end the day of rejoicing. The celebrations will have begun with a united Service on the Recreation Ground on the previous Sunday and the day itself will begin with Holy Communion in the Parish Church."

### The Library                                                       April 1953

"The branch of the County Library now established in our Parish Hall is proving very popular, there being over six hundred members."

### Highcliffe Community Centre                                    March 1959

"Failure to acquire Culmore House as a Community Centre has not prevented the Committee from pursuing its plans. By this time most of the readers have doubtless seen the display in Mr. W.E. Pepper's shop window,

Lymington Road, of the various arts and crafts that could be pursued at a Community Centre. The Chairman informs us that she has been promised the support of the Highcliffe Orchestra, the art class, the chess club, the Castle Documentary Film Club, the Hants 122 detachment of the Red Cross, the old time dancing club, even before any building has been acquired and the Committee is prepared to consider starting classes in a variety of subjects. The Committee will open subscription lists when a suitable building site has been found."

## The Highcliffe Citizens Association                                October 1959

"The Highcliffe Citizens Association have once again performed a very useful service in spotlighting the use of beach huts on our cliffs for sleeping purposes. To have secured over 1,600 elector's signatures for their petition is no mean achievement and shows how much feeling there is in Highcliffe on the subject. Many arguments against the use of the huts have been brought forward but nowhere have we seen reference to the moral aspect. For whole families, parents and children of both sexes, and all agree to be living together completely without privacy, seems to the writer to be undesirable in every way. Such living conditions are more reminiscent of life in a refugee camp than in 20th century England."

(The Council finally agreed to end the use of beach huts for sleeping purposes and within a few years afterwards most of the day huts had disappeared because of erosion and subsidence of the cliffs.)

## April 1960

"Ringwood Road is due to be widened and improvements provided during the 1960/61 financial year. The first section to be dealt with is that between Elphinstone Road and Amberwood Cottage."

## October 1960

"The Borough Surveyor tells us that plans are nearing completion for the improvement of Hinton Wood Avenue from Ice House Hill to Lymington Road. On the Wolhayes Convent side, a woodland path will meander in and out of the trees, on the Vicarage side the roadway will be made safe by the removal of the bulge of the Vicarage boundary midway between the house and the Church gate."

## November 1960

"The Highcliffe Community Association was founded following a public meeting in May 1960 and will, in due course, benefit to the extent of a £400 gift from the Highcliffe Festival of 1960 and hopes to secure premises or a site for the centre. Activities, which include several which began in a very small way four years ago, immediately expanded upon the association being formed and, with the help of its membership of 260, now cover a wide range of subjects."

## March 1961

"The new library, 290 Lymington Road, is behind Diana's premises, the entrance being between that shop and the Co-operative Stores. Mr. Golding, the Librarian at Christchurch, states that the opening date will be early in March."

## April 1961

"When Highcliffe's new library was opened a tribute was paid to the past services of Mr. K. Whitcombe and Mrs. Holding, who had been part-time librarians for so long. Mr. Whitcombe having been first employed in 1937. If we have a criticism to make it is that the two small rooms give the library a somewhat cramped effect and it would certainly be somewhat inconvenient to supply a table and chair, where one could make notes of the reference section. Apart from that, the library has many new books and is bright and cheerful."

## October 1961

"The name of Ice House Hill for the rise at Hinton Wood Avenue and junction of Nea Road is almost forgotten in Highcliffe. The entrance to the old Ice House, which gave the Hill its name, was unexpectedly revealed when workmen removed trees and levelled the ground at the triangle during the alterations at this dangerous spot. There is nothing new about freezing as a method of preserving foodstuffs. In the days before mechanical refrigeration many landowners constructed large pits on their estate, in which quantities of river ice were placed during the winter. Such an ice house was that whose bricks have probably now been seen for the last time and one more link with the past will survive only as long as its fading name."

(There has been mentioned previously the completion of the Methodist's building programme of a new hall [1962] and church [1963], together with the opening of the new Highcliffe Junior School [1963].)

## March 1962

"Christchurch Borough Council are to be congratulated on the old people's bungalows, Gordon Mount, in Chewton Common Road."

105

PAGE OF ADVERTS FROM PARISH MAGAZINE 1888

## April 1962

"Wharncliffe Road was recently made up by the Borough Council and is now almost unrecognisable. The surface, made up to the Council's specification, is admirable and makes a trip to the cliff top at Highcliffe very much more pleasant than it formerly was."

## January 1964

"Some months ago Miss Iris Shipman came to me with an idea she had about the medical loan department, which has been housed at Hoburne since 1945 and which she has run from there since that date. Last winter's great freeze up had brought home to her how very out of the way Hoburne was for such a depot and how very easily it could become non-functionable in such weather, which was just the last thing one would want in such circumstances. Among the many activities which the late Mrs. Balfour was associated with was the British Red Cross Society. When she was asked if the local branch of the organisation could house a medical loan department she asked her brother, Brigadier General Browne, if he would allow one of the rooms at Hoburne for this purpose. He very kindly gave his consent and Miss Shipman, who was the founder Commandant of Hants 122, undertook to run the depot.

After Mrs. Balfour's death, those nearest to her felt that, in view of the many kindnesses she had done during her lifetime, some kind of memorial should be created. This is where Miss Shipman thought of a building that could be used to house a medical loans depot, situated in a place convenient for everyone and which would not be cut off in bad weather, when it was needed, and now Mr. Stanley Kermode enters the picture. Very generously he offered a site adjoining Greystones in Waterford Road on which to erect a building not exceeding £300."

## May 1965

"Good wishes to Councillor Mrs. I.A. Stevenson for her term of office as Mayor of the ancient Borough of Christchurch."

## May 24th 1965

"The new building of the Highcliffe Men's Club was opened by Councillor Mrs. I. Stevenson at the beginning of her mayoral year. The new building consists of a large hall with a stage, a bar, a lounge and a billiard room and cost £16,000."

## June 1965

"The first issue of this magazine published in January 1888, carried an advertisement for the one shop then established in this village, Frampton

Brothers of the Post Office, Newtown. Over the years the Frampton family have served us well as sub-postmasters and mistresses and to the recently retired member of the family our thanks are now due."

## September 1965

"The demolition of Kimber's shop is, I believe, the end of the ancient hamlet of Slop Pond, the name by which the few dwellings there were known before Newtown swallowed them up and when Highcliffe was the name of the big house only. The name of Newtown is perpetuated in the well known guest house, but I have so far been unsuccessful in persuading anyone to bring back into use the ancient name. Perhaps Slop Pond Buildings or Slop Pond Garage would not sound quite right."

The Parish Magazine recalls an important date when the Queen and Prince Philip visited Christchurch and drove through Highcliffe on their way to complete one of many tours of the country.

## August 1966

"Highcliffe has had many royal visitors in the past. None of these Royal visitors of yesteryear could have received a warmer welcome than that given to the Queen and Duke of Edinburgh on the occasion of their recent drive through Highcliffe. The Lymington Road was lined from end to end and with the children of St. Marks School, all 245 of them, waving a Union Jack, he or she had made in preparation for this exciting day."

The old Vicarage at the junction of the Lymington Road and Hinton Wood Avenue was sold for £22,500 in 1966. It was about 104 years since the first Vicar had moved in there. The new Vicarage, 'Woodlea', is in Nea Road. The new Parish Hall, adjacent to the Church, was opened in 1968.

The local Scouts had had a variety of venues from the Vicarage stables, the Parish hall, a Nissen hut behind the Hall, but in 1969 their own headquarters were opened at the Scout Hut in Chewton Common Road – the land being leased for a peppercorn rent from the Meyrick estate.

As previously mentioned the Roman Catholic Church and St. Mark's Infant School were both opened during the year 1969.

There seemed to be a need at this time for further recreational facilities and in 1975 the Highcliffe Bowling Club was formed on a magnificent site, quite unique in bowling circles, in Nea Meadow. The Club was opened in July by the Mayor of Christchurch, Councillor John Morgan. The anniversary of the opening is marked each year by 'President's Day'.

Before 1932, the local government of the village was exercised by the Highcliffe Parish Council (part of Christchurch Rural District). Highcliffe then became No. 4 Ward of the Municipal Borough of Christchurch with three representatives on the Council. By 1971 No. 4 Ward had many more electors than any of the other wards within the Borough and a decision was taken to divide it into two wards, Highcliffe East and Highcliffe West, to give the area representation on the Council more commensurate with its population. Three councillors were elected for each ward. After 1974 there was a further rearrangement of wards following Local Government Reorganisation establishing Nea Ward (2 councillors), Wingfield Ward (2 councillors) and Chewton Ward (3 councillors).

Councillor Mrs. Irene Stevenson, a resident of Highcliffe for many years and a long serving member of the Council was honoured in 1981 by the award of honorary freeman of the Borough of Christchurch.

The following figures show the growth of Highcliffe during the last seventy years. The figures indicate the Highcliffe electorate: -

| 1935 | 1,432 | 1970 | 7,282 |
|------|-------|------|-------|
| 1945 | 1,980 | 1975 | 7,976 |
| 1950 | 2,474 | 1981 | 8,718 |
| 1955 | 3,031 | 1985 | 10,640 |
| 1960 | 3,610 | 1990 | 10,900 |
| 1965 | 4,991 | 1995 | 11,150 |

During the latter part of the 20th century many familiar landmarks have disappeared. The British Legion Hall was replaced by Homecliffe House; The Highcliffe Hotel was replaced by The Lawns; the beautiful old house, Chewton Lodge, was demolished and a small housing estate built. Waterford House and the fields behind where the horses grazed have been developed with blocks of flats and houses.

# WHAT OF THE FUTURE ... ?

In the first edition of this book published in 1981 Mr. D. Pratley, Dip.T.P., M.R.T.P.I., the Planning Officer for Christchurch, indicated what he envisaged would happen in the village. It is reproduced here word for word as it makes for interesting reading: -

"The land bounded by Hoburne Lane, Highcliffe Road and Lyndhurst Road is already in process of being developed with a number of small houses for the first-time buyers and a few larger properties for those in the middle income bracket. The density of the housing will be relieved by the provision of extensive open spaces.

The land at Steamer Point, so long held by the Ministry of Defence, has now been vacated and designated as an area for development, e.g. with luxury houses, for public access and perhaps for natural history educational purposes, supervised by a warden. These questions are awaiting decision by the Secretary of State for the Environment.

Erosion by the sea which became serious in the nineteen fifties was brought under control by the construction of a wooden revetment with groynes. For the future coast protection, reliance may very well be placed on a beach replenishment scheme, i.e. the use of special equipment to suck up sand from the seabed and pump it on to the shore, building up the sand level on the beach. Notwithstanding the protection of the toe of the cliff there was a continuing problem of subsidence of the soft clay and sand of which the cliff is formed but drainage works have enabled vegetation to become re-established.

The subsidence of parts of Chewton Bunny through which the Walkford Brook flows, has been a worry to those living near. Culverting of the stream and other works have been undertaken and in future it is proposed to stabilize the riverbed by constructing a lake and weir at the southern end of the Bunny. This will, hopefully, add another attractive feature to this part of the coast.

The traffic congestion in Lymington Road has proved a serious problem recently and there have been plans for a Highcliffe By-Pass, north of the Lymington Road for many years. Unfortunately, such a solution awaits an improvement in the financial climate of the country.

Perhaps however, it is the Castle itself which will play the major role in the development of Highcliffe as a community over the next few years. Although only a skeleton now remains of its former grandeur, it is a stark reminder of how and where the village of Highcliffe began. Now the Castle ruins are undergoing a renaissance as a local place of recreation and historical interest and this, together with the gradual winning of the battle against cliff erosion means that within a few years Highcliffe could once again become a popular resort."

# Chapter Eleven

# HIGHCLIFFE CASTLE II

*"Some day the Castle will make a beautiful and interesting ruin,"* Mrs Stuart
Wortley *remarked to Lord Abingdon and me, one early summer's evening some
thirty years ago. We both laughed and teased her with questions about whose ghost
would glide among the cold, moss-covered stone, the crumbling rubble: but
occasionally, remembering it, we would talk about it, speculating on the Castle's
future in a changing world.*

*An extract from 'Highcliffe Castle' by Tahu Hole  (1972)*

HIGHCLIFFE CASTLE BEFORE RESTORATION

In 1977 Christchurch Council purchased the neglected Grade I listed
Highcliffe Castle for £65,000. The grounds were to be preserved as a public open
space with access to the beach and car parking for one hundred cars.

The Grade I listing meant that the building was of special Architectural and
Historic interest and was the finest example of Romantic and Picturesque style of

111

architecture which flourished in the early part of the 19th century. It is now the most important building of its sort in the country if not Europe.

The official Opening Ceremony took place on Saturday, June 4th 1977 when the Mayor of Christchurch, Cllr. John Beauchamp, formally declared the grounds open to the public. On this day, too, the whole country was celebrating the Silver Jubilee of Queen Elizabeth ll.

There were Morris dancing, folk singing, art and craft stalls and flower displays. On Sunday the Highcliffe churches held a united Service on the recreation ground when the preacher was the Lord Bishop of Southampton, Rt. Rev. John Cavel M.A. On Monday, there was more dancing. children's sports and Army displays, followed on Tuesday with a Grand Carnival Procession of floats through the village. The celebrations concluded with a bonfire and fireworks on the cliffs.

English Heritage had been concerned for some time about the Castle and in 1988 joined with Christchurch Council in commissioning architects, Niall Phillips to produce a feasibility study into the future use of the crumbling Castle.

At a public meeting at Mudeford Wood Community Centre Mr Niall Phillips gave the following options: –

1. Demolish the Castle at an estimated cost of £500,000
2. Retain the Castle as a ruin at an estimated cost of £1.2m
3. Conserve the Castle at an estimated cost of £2.5m
4. Convert the Castle into luxury apartments, hotel, or offices

## 1989

A group of Highcliffe residents formed The Friends of Highcliffe Castle Action Group with the aim of promoting the Castle. Exhibitions concerning the history of the Castle; the Stuart Wortley family; the life of Lady Waterford; the links between the Castle and the village; and the fascinating architecture of the Castle were mounted at various venues to arouse interest.

## 1989 - 90

The Council decided to conduct a public consultation to hear the comments of the Highcliffe residents about the future of the Castle. A document was produced and public meetings held giving everyone the chance to express their views. There were many people who opposed the proposal to repair the Castle who made their opinions known through the local papers and at meetings.

## March 1990

The results of the consultation were considered by the Council – by the end of the year protection work of cocooning the building in scaffolding and plastic to protect it from the elements was completed and a temporary roof was constructed.

Christchurch Council agreed to English Heritage's demands to share 50% of the £360,000 cost of the emergency work.

## June 1990

Niall Phillips invited the Friends of Highcliffe Castle to help in the retrieval of some of the artefacts from the interior rubble of the Castle. These were safely stored and used in the restoration programme. Some were too damaged but were used as patterns for new stonework.

## February 1992

The Council agreed in principle to the idea of building on 13 acres of Highcliffe golf course to fund the restoration of the Castle. The plans were to build a retirement village of 200 homes there. The Golf Club would then move to Chewton Farm. This idea fell through because of the volume of objections: problems with planning application and the final straw, the drop in land values.

## April 1992

The Friends of Highcliffe Castle Action Group opened the tearooms with the help of volunteer staff.

## 1994   Restoration Programme:

The Castle was to be restored in four phases. Each of the first three phases would be funded equally between Christchurch Council and English Heritage.

**Phase 1.** The Visitors' Centre in the Winter Garden – to be completed 1994

**Phase 2.** New windows, re-roofing the Library, Octagon, Ante Library and the Drawing Room – to be completed August 1995

**Phase 3.** Repairs to the Penleaze Rooms, the East Tower – to be completed June 1997

**Phase 4.** Complete external repairs, Great Hall, the interior of the Octagon, new mains services, relocate toilets, refurbish grounds, improve car park and access road – to be paid for from Lottery Fund – to be completed 1998.

## January 1995

The Highcliffe Castle Charitable Trust (HCCT) was founded incorporating some of The Friends and representatives from Christchurch Council. A bid was made by the Council and supported by HCCT for Heritage Lottery funding of £2.6m, which if successful would fund Phase 4.

During this time a permanent exhibition of the history of the Castle was displayed in the Visitors' Centre in the Winter Garden. About forty volunteers ran the shop, acted as guides to the Castle and helped with the various exhibitions.

These included workshops, art and craft exhibitions and a flower festival.

The Visitors Centre was opened on June 9th by Lord Montagu of Beaulieu who arrived in the same 1899 Daimler 12hp which carried the Prince of Wales, the future Edward VII, around Highcliffe in 1900.

In June, too, *The Times* carried the headline, 'Lottery pays out £2.6m to restore castle' – continued restoration assured.

HIGHCLIFFE CASTLE DURING RESTORATION

## December 1998

In October the scaffolding which had surrounded the Castle came down.

It was during this year that the beautiful north window was brought back to the Castle and installed in the Great Hall. The stained glass from the window had been safely stored with Kings, a glazier in Norwich. The window, dated 1547, is called the Jesse window because it details the family tree of Jesus Christ who descended from Jesse. The HCCT raised the extra £35,000 needed to restore the window into the renovated stonework by the sale of redundant stone and profits from the Visitors Centre and the Tea Rooms and donations. Special diamond panes at the base of the window were inscribed with the names of donors who raised over £500.

In 1998 too, the heraldic stag was returned to stand guard over the Great Portico entrance to the Castle.

RESTORED GRAND PORTICO

The keys of the Castle were formally handed over to the Mayor of Christchurch, Cllr. John Lofts by the Chairman of Linfords, the main contractor, on the completion of all the exterior work.

## 1999

Following a suggestion by HCCT, Christchurch Council applied and obtained a licence to hold wedding ceremonies at the Castle. (In 1999 there were six weddings – in 2003 there were 120 weddings.)

The marble statue of Lady Waterford by Sir Joseph Boehm was returned to the Castle, a generous gift from Dorset County Council, after an absence of thirty years. The statue had stood in Christchurch Library but when the repairs at the Castle were finished she returned home.

In April the Council officially took over the management of the Castle, and Visitors' Centre from the HCCT. Christchurch Council seconded its Policy and PR member, Mike Allen, to manage the Castle and together with the volunteers (and a small staff) managed the Centre and its grounds.

## July 2000   The Jesse Window

It was fitting that the ceremony to 'open' the window to the public view took place in the millennium year of Christ's birth, July 2000. The window was rededicated by ministers of the local churches. The remaining three Trustees presented the cheque of £35,000 to the Council. Then, their patron, Lord Montagu, declared, "this window to be open, but as that is a physical impossibility, I declare the window open to view by all."

This very moving occasion was the fitting finale to the many years of work by The Friends, HCCT and others in the community to ensure that the Council fulfilled its obligations to this important building.

Between **2000 – 2003** a great deal happened. Visitor figures rose to over 40,000 a year. More rooms were brought into the Visitors' Centre and all the fences were taken down.

What a contrast from the crumbling ruin of 1977! The Castle in 2003 is alive with activity, changing exhibitions, concerts, a gift shop, open-air events on the lawns and tearooms to provide the visitor with light refreshments. Confidence in the Castle allowed the Council to apply for a further £2.1m from the Heritage Lottery towards a further phase of repairs. This unfortunately was not granted.

# Chapter Twelve

## THE VILLAGE 1970 – 2003

### 1973 Highcliffe Friends in Need.

A group of people from the Highcliffe churches met to discuss the growing need for organised voluntary help in Highcliffe to meet some of the needs for the less able folk in the area.

A formal meeting drew up the constitution and it was agreed that five co-ordinators would be available in the mornings Monday to Friday to take requests for help and to pass them on to volunteers. The most usual requests were for assistance with transport to hospitals and doctor's appointments, the chemist with urgent prescriptions and also for folk to sit with vulnerable people whilst their carers went out. (At the time of writing this work is still continuing.)

### 1979 - 80 The Highcliffe Citizens Journal

The Council proposes to build a new car park near Jesmond Avenue but there had been such a storm of protest that the proposal was shelved until parking in Highcliffe was considered as a whole.

The Council has been anxious to discover what views Highcliffe residents had concerning development on the cliff face; specifically should there be huts available for letting and sale. It was decided to carry out a referendum of all residents.

### July 1981 Highcliffe Community Association.

At this time the Community Association was growing and badly in need of permanent premises. Greystones, a 19th century listed building was owned by the Christchurch Old Peoples Housing Association and had been used as a rest home. The building was in need of extensive repairs. A Trust was formed between the Christchurch Old Peoples Housing Association and the Highcliffe Community Association each contributing £20,000 towards the repairs. Each would nominate four trustees and the Trust would lease Greystones at a net rent of £1,200 a year for the next 40 years.

### July 1983  Highcliffe Castle Golf Club.

A new clubhouse costing £225,000 was opened at Highcliffe Golf Club by Mr John Jacobs. This clubhouse was paid for by the 350 members of the Golf Club.

### September 1983  Day Care Centre.

A purpose built Day Care Centre for the Borough of Christchurch was opened on part of the site of the old school in Lymington Road. The building cost £500,000. Its purpose was primarily to give support to frail and elderly people so that they could live in their own homes and postpone the time when they would need residential accommodation.

The kitchens were designed to provide meals on wheels and laundry facilities were provided for home helps. About 70 people attended the Day Centre each day and the premises were available for other purposes in the evenings.

## 1985 Silverways Nursing Home

The Christchurch Housing Association (formally Christchurch Housing and Welfare Association) built a large nursing home costing £1,000,000 and said to be the second largest in the country. This was opened on completion of the transfer of Greystones to the Community Association.

HEILA HOUSE

## 1986 Heila House.

A large new medical centre for the Highcliffe Group Practice was built next to the Day Centre at 248 Lymington Road. This replaced a much smaller centre at 280 Lymington Road.

118

**October 16th 1987 Hurricane.**

A disastrous hurricane struck the South of England causing widespread damage. The flats on the coast were badly affected and the roofs of the old people's flats in Greystones, Waterford Road, were torn off in the early hours of the morning. However local residents came to the rescue and in time the damage was repaired.

**1988 Public Consultation.**

Niall Phillips Architects were commissioned by Christchurch Council and English Heritage to carry out a feasibility study into the future of Highcliffe Castle.

**1990 Crow's Nest Café on the Cliff Top.**

A young man lost control of the car he was driving and drove into the Crow's Nest Café setting it on fire.

Although this happened in 1990 the Crow's Nest has never been replaced.

CROWS NEST CAFÉ

**1990 - 91 St. Mark's Church.**

A large building project, initiated by Rev. John Seaford, costing £450,000 was completed. The architect, Richard Scott designed an extension round the outside of the existing church, making the church the centre of activity.

A new porch with glass doors now separates the nave from the entrance porch. The round stained glass window by Henry Haig was specially commissioned and depicts the Christian journey of life. The old organ loft/gallery was replaced by a new gallery and staircase.

Ancillary rooms were built along the north wall to link with the vestry. In the space between the hall and the church a library and office were built.

On 11th August 1991, on completion of the work, the Bishop of Southampton rededicated the church.

### 1992 Newtown - Highcliffe

It is one hundred years since the name of the village as Newtown was discarded and the village took on the name of the Highcliffe estate and the house became Highcliffe Castle.

### 1994 Heritage Lottery Fund

Highcliffe Castle restoration was assured with the grant of £2.6m from the Heritage Lottery Fund.

### 1996 Highcliffe By Pass.

The Highcliffe Relief Road, having been discussed for over 60 years, when it was the northern boundary of the village, was removed from the Local Plan and the land designated a green corridor.

THE GLOBE HIGHCLIFFE c.1908
(The Stable Block is next to the Globe)

## 1999 The Stable Block

The one hundred year old stable block alongside the Globe Inn was in a dangerous condition. The Globe's owners, Whitbread, met with The Highcliffe Stables Community Trust who wanted to restore the building and use it as an exhibition centre. It was hoped the restoration would be funded by a lottery grant. The Trust had worked hard to make this a valuable asset to the village. But on investigation the structure of the stable block would not support the extensive alterations needed.

## 1999 Skateboard Park

The lack of leisure facilities for the youth of Highcliffe was causing problems. The need was for a skateboard park – sites suggested were Chewton Bunny, Highcliffe Recreation Ground, Chewton Common and the cliff top.

## 2000 The Stable Block

The stables of the Globe Inn were demolished and a small garden planted. The two seats were donated by the Highcliffe Residents Association and the Highcliffe Community Association.

## 2001 Cliff Top

The Christchurch Leisure Committee voted to seek outline planning permission for a facility on the cliff top to replace the old Crow's Nest Café.

## March 2002 Village Green Status

Highcliffe Residents Association submitted an application for Village Green Status for the Highcliffe cliff top so that the general public have free access to the lovely coastline views.

## June 4th 2002 The Golden Jubilee Celebrations

Highcliffe celebrated the Queen's Golden Jubilee in the grounds of Highcliffe Castle. It was designed as a typical English afternoon with a concert by the Highcliffe Band, exhibitions, stalls and a line up of classic cars. Entrance to the Castle was free and the Tea Rooms provided Jubilee Cream Teas.

In **August** there was a spontaneous demonstration by 150 members and friends of the Highcliffe Residents Association in support of the Village Green proposal. This proposal was later opposed by Christchurch Council and refused by Dorset County Council as the land was already adequately protected by Government legislation and the disadvantage of such a proposal outweighed the advantage as had been proved by the Council elsewhere in the Borough. (Barrack Road recreation ground.)

The Council undertook a Borough wide character assessment which went to public consultation in order to protect and control density and height of buildings in the area which is very important to Highcliffe as it also protects green areas and cliffs.

## March 2003

Stuart Lodge Hotel in Waterford Road was demolished making room for a block of flats following permission granted by a Government Inspector on appeal.

STUART LODGE HOTEL

# REMINISCENCES

*Many years ago the author travelled round Highcliffe with a tape recorder talking to some of the people who had lived in Highcliffe for many years. The following is a transcript of part of those conversations.*

### MR. HARRY LEE – A butcher in the village for many years.

*How far back can you remember?*

About 50 odd years connected to the Castle. The owners were General Stuart Wortley and Mrs. Stuart Wortley. He was a retired general and she was a Guthrie, the bankers, very educated, a very nice person indeed.

*Were they part of the village?*

Oh yes! She celebrated her 80th birthday and I will show you the card she sent me, - "Highcliffe Castle. Thank you for coming to my 80th birthday party, for your help and for your gift and your cheers. VSW. 1866-1946"

SEA CORNER (Now G & T's)

*Tell me about the shops in the village.*

They were nearly all Framptons in Highcliffe at that time. The Post Master was a Frampton; the barber was a Frampton; the grocer was a Frampton; the two builders were Framptons; and the baker was a Frampton, he had 5 sons. Now there is only one left – Dennis who used to be a barber. They used to have a football team of Framptons at one time in Highcliffe and Jose in Bransgore had nine or ten sons and they had a football team. It was a real Derby day when Highcliffe played Bransgore. We made our own amusements then with singing, football and we had a band – The Highcliffe Silver Band.

It was started by Colonel Honey who lived at The Pines in Walkford. When I joined it was called The Highcliffe Silver Band. The old chap who used to teach us was a retired policeman who took up boot making in the village. Later his son took over. Weir was their name. There is nowhere you can buy a pair of shoes now in Highcliffe. Mr Anders up the road was another boot maker and Mr Bailey, who I worked with; his father was a boot maker. He made me a pair of boots. They cost about 12 bob – that was 1930.

*What do you remember about the war years?*

It was pretty quiet here – not much going on. Did you know the German Ambassador, Sir William Goshen, lived at Beacon Lodge when war broke out? He used to drive a horse and wagonette up to the village otherwise Alf Adams, his coachman, would drive him. Alf was a tall man with a slight limp. He fell out of an apple tree and broke his neck.

*Could you go down to the beach during the war?*

No, because it was mined. I used to go along with a policeman because I was a special constable and he knew where to go.

We used to go round the village at night. When the siren went we had to go out. One night we went to a hotel in Holdenhurst Road in Bournemouth where American soldiers were billeted. We were first on the scene before the Bournemouth constables. There were seven of us then and I am the only one left.

*Did you ever meet Gordon Selfridge when he lived in Highcliffe?*

It was during the war that Gordon Selfridge had the Castle. The family came down at weekends. He was going to build a house on Hengistbury Head but his wife died.

When he used to come down to the Castle at Christmas he used to give the children a treat in the Parish Hall with Christmas tree and presents. One year Mrs. Selfridge went to give the prizes and she stood by the back door and caught a chill and died. She's buried in St. Mark's churchyard and so was Gordon Selfridge. The graves down there are looked after by the firm because Gordon Selfridge never had any money.

He had two daughters and they both married Russians who had no money so he had to keep them as well. One of the daughters used to come to stay with us. My wife's mother kept a boarding house in Wortley Road – the first house there. Prince Ruzenski and Princess Ruzenski brought Tattiana down with her nanny to stay.

## MRS. EDNA MACFADYEN – wife of the Town Clerk of Christchurch.

I remember Culmore – Mrs. Wallace Power lived there and she was quite the lady of the village when we came in December 1953. She was very tall and elegant, Irish and scatty but full of good works and into everything. She had garden parties at Culmore each summer for charities and everybody in the village went. She was President of the Bournemouth Shakespeare Society so they gave open-air performances in her garden. She was very keen on 'The Band' as she called Bournemouth Symphony Orchestra.

We had sold our old car before we came here so were without a new one for a few months. So Mrs. Wallace Power said, "Any time you want the car James is there for the asking." James was her chauffer. You can imagine how intimidating that was. A powerful wealthy woman putting her chauffeur at our disposal – "James will come and collect you."

She was Mayor of Christchurch for two years; National Vice President of the RSPCA; she was a JP and a County Councillor.

She had a huge concert one evening when she had Charles Groves, later Sir Charles Groves to conduct 'The Band'.

She died whilst walking in The Paddock. (The land opposite Culmore since developed as Elmwood Way.) She was very highly regarded and there is a seat to her memory at the end of Castle Avenue.

*Which church did you attend?*

The Methodist Church was the Cinderella church of the village. The vicar was amazed that the new Town Clerk was a Methodist. It was a really poor church. Rev. Jukes was the Minister. He was well over 70. He was very thoughtful in his preaching and very gentle but he couldn't do much because he was so frail. Mrs. Lunn was the organist for many years.

Then Mr. and Mrs. Eric Bedford arrived and Mr. and Mrs. Sam Wheatly who were very wealthy, all three daughters went to Roedean School. Mrs. Wheatley used to say to me, "You are looking very tired. When my children were as young as yours I took 3 months off and went on holiday."

They were the first people who settled in Highcliffe who had not been here for years. So they brought new ideas and Mr. Wheatley used to stroll around the village in his plus-fours and stick referring to the Methodist Church as 'Knight's Tabernacle' – meaning that the Methodist Church was run by Mr. and Mrs. Knight!

It was at this time that the estates were being sold and developed. When Rev. Greg Carter arrived he decided that no one coming to live in the new bungalows would come to the church as it was then. So he planned a new church that would attract people.

## MISS ELLWOOD – District Nurse, daughter of Horatio Ellwood the Headmaster. She was a Catholic.

When I first came here after my training as a District Nurse and Midwife my area was really Somerford but there were only four houses there then so I was given Burton and Holmsley.

We were known as the Parish Nurses until the National Health Service started in 1948. At that time there was the Highcliffe Nursing Association with Mrs. Wallace Power as treasurer. We collected money from the patients, what we thought they could afford – two pounds for the first baby and one pound for the second and third and for general work it was half a crown or one shilling. This money was not our salary, which was paid from Winchester, but was paid to the Highcliffe Nursing Association – possibly for dressings etc. I used to go to the Holmsley gypsies. They always had the money ready on the mantelpiece waiting for you. They never owed a penny!

The first nurse I remember as a child was old Nurse Lock who lived in Elphinstone Road during the First World War. She recognised my spots as chicken pox! Later Nurse Sherwood came to live in Bracken Way.

*Can you remember when the Castle was a private residence?*

The Claretians bought the Castle in 1953 before that it was a rather a doubtful school. When I returned to Highcliffe in 1948 we used to live in Rothesay Drive and we were very friendly with the Claretians. We knew them all well. Father Banano was the first principal but not very good. When the Claretians first came there were novices; the little boy postulates came later and finally students came from Birmingham. When they dispersed one stayed on for six months as he was a Spaniard and ran the Spanish Club in Bournemouth. He used to come back to sleep in the Castle every night on his own. What a brave man!

The Claretians had no money when they came. I well remember an Ordination Service when the Bishop came and there were no plates or cutlery and half of the residents of Rothesay Drive provided plates and food that night. I knew John Harvey, the Bishop was fond of raw onions, so I took a plate of raw onions over to the Castle. He was thrilled.

*Tell me about the old school.*

My father lived in the little house next to the school and my sister was born in the room at the top. Then they built the house, Moorfields for him and he stayed there until his [second] wife died. Then he built six houses in Lymington Road opposite John Ridout's [now Regent House] and lived at Number 36.

The school building hasn't changed very much. A cloakroom has been added. There were three classrooms and three teachers. Miss Astridge took the infants and there was Miss Phillips. Children used to come from Highcliffe, Chewton, Walkford and Gus. Children used to walk all the way over Gus Common to the school. The families from there did not have very good reputations. My father would only let me sit next to the clean ones. There was a mother who was known as a 'twicer' because she always had twins. I don't know how many she had! My father retired in 1923 and he died in 1924.

## MRS. LUNN – wife of the manager of Elliotts, Outfitters and Tailors, in the village, a resident and a member of the Methodist Church.

*Where did you live?*

We lived above the shop at 416, (now Saffron) Lymington Road near the bus stop. My husband came to Highcliffe in 1925 as the first manager of this new branch of Elliotts of Lymington. I and our new baby, Jean, joined him there later in the year. At first there was no main drainage and the cart used to come round to empty people's cesspits. They were peculiar drainage arrangements and I was horrified.

*Did you know John and Mary Frampton who did so much for the little Methodist Chapel?*

Mr. and Mrs. Frampton lived next door to the Chapel in Grace Villa (Bertie's Fish & chip shop) and where the Hall is now was his back garden where all our bazaars were held.

We had choir practice in Mr. Frampton's front room. We all sat on the settee and practised singing Sankey hymns which we used to sing during the collection. The Framptons had no children but Mrs. Frampton was very fond of singing. It was a very lively church then in the country tradition. The church held about sixty people and there was often no need to play the harmonium, as the singing was so strong it filled the church. The congregation was not made up of retired folk as it is now; most members were in business or worked in shops.

*Was the village very different from now?*

The beach and the cliffs were lovely. The beach itself was more extensive than it is now and the tide did not completely cover it. There were beach huts on the cliffs and they were a great worry in winter. They were always slipping particularly if there were gales. It was a joy for us to have a beach hut as we lived upstairs over the shop and our long back garden was occupied by chickens, beehives and apple trees.

When war came we had to take the huts up. That is why they disappeared. We were not allowed down there. We dismantled our hut and took everything up except the doors. When we went back next day the doors had disappeared. Father and I searched the beach and found they had been used as a roof for a dug out. The soldiers had been busy. They were billeted at Stuart Lodge. We could hear the Sergeant Major drilling them each morning.

**MISS ASTRIDGE AND SISTER WINIFRED GILES** – both ladies taught for a number of years in the village school. Sister Winifred was also a Wesley Deaconess.

*Were there any evacuees at the school during the war?*

During the war an emergency kitchen was set up in the school playground. When the siren sounded the children went into the trenches which had been dug in the woods (where the path cuts through to Imber Drive). We didn't spend very long in there but one afternoon we were there from 3 o'clock until a quarter to six. The children were very good; we tried to get them to go to the toilet before they went into the trenches. Once there we used to sing and have competitions. We had to wait for the 'All Clear' before we could leave the trenches. We had a lot of evacuees from Southampton and Portsmouth. The school worked part time because we couldn't get all the children in.

**LOU STRICKLAND B.E.M.** – worked on the cliffs for Highcliffe Parish Council and for Christchurch Borough Council

*In the School Log there are several entries each year in January when the children went 'tapping'. What was that?*

I think the 'tapping' must mean beating – the shooting season was from October 1st to February 1st, the last gun cleaning was January 23rd. Maybe they were children of Sir George Meyrick's tenants in which case he would have them out.

*Tell me about your work.*

I have worked for 46 years on Highcliffe cliffs. I worked when it was Highcliffe Parish Council before Christchurch took over. There were four of us working there and I was the youngest and had to do all the running about from one end of the cliffs to the other and up and down the steps all day long.

When Christchurch took over there were 601 chalets on the cliffs. There were three terraces of them from the Bunny to Culmore. My work involved general maintenance of the cliffs, drainage of the cliffs, putting up and taking down chalets and painting them. I got stuck many times in the thick mud on the cliffs. I lost my boots and had to walk home to get another pair so that I could dig out the lost ones! Anyone could die down there; it was really treacherous in winter. Anyone who got stuck up to their knees in the mud and started to struggle – they'd only got to fall backwards or forwards and they were finished. I always said, the best thing to do if you were caught like that was to stand still and shout. I used to take a plank down with me and then crawl along and dig round the person and then lever them out. I lent forward and got them to put their arms round my neck and then I would pull. There was a loud squelch. No shoes on when they were pulled out. It is much safer now although it is still a bit tricky below Beacon Lodge.

When you get the rain falling continuously on the cliffs, the clay oozes out at the base of the cliff spewing it out but was contained by the revetment which had been built along the beach. So when you are walking there you are really walking on clay.

HIGHCLIFFE BEACH c.1930

*Tell me about the bridge crossing the Bunny on the main road?*

The first bridge across the Bunny was put there by me and my mate. The Christchurch and Lymington boundary was in the middle of the stream. We put the bridge across because neither Christchurch nor Lymington Councils were prepared to put a bridge there.

*What about your B.E.M.?*

Someone local recommended me – it wasn't the Council. It was awarded in 1976/7, Jubilee year and she (the Queen) was abroad and I had it presented by the Lord Lieutenant of Dorset down in Christchurch. I was given a medal and letter explaining that owing to one thing and another she could not present it herself. It was awarded for meritorious service.

# APPENDIX A

# Officiating Clergy of the Village of Highcliffe

## ST. MARK'S CHURCH

| Vicar | Date | Patron |
|---|---|---|
| John Dobson | Priest-in-Charge | |
| Albert Aitkin | 1838-1843 | Lady Stuart de Rothesay |
| Robert Pinckney, M.A. | 1871-1879 | Lady Waterford |
| Thomas Lindon, M.A. | 1879-1887 | Lady Waterford |
| Samuel Filleul, M.A. | 1887-1889 | Lady Waterford |
| Algernon Ryder, M.A. | 1889-1895 | Lady Waterford |
| Edward Carpenter, M.A. | 1895-1908 | Gen. Stuart Wortley |
| Frederick Gray, M.A. | 1908-1919 | Gen. Stuart Wortley |
| Frederick Evans, B.A. | 1919-1925 | Gen. Stuart Wortley |
| Charles Gould, M.A. | 1925-1943 | Gen. Stuart Wortley |
| Henry Brownlow, B.A., B.Sc. | 1943-1952 | The Bishop (by lapse) |
| Robert Barnett, M.A. | 1952-1978 | Oxford University |
| John Seaford, B.A. DIP.TH. | 1978-1994 | Sir George Meyrick |
| John Williams | 1994-2003 | Bishop of Winchester |

## THE METHODIST CHURCH

*Ministers*

| | | |
|---|---|---|
| 1891 | Rev. George Birch | Poole Circuit |
| 1907 | Rev. J. Wellings | |
| | Rev. Kennedy | |
| 1925 | Rev. William Musson | *Bournemouth First Station* |
| | Rev. Ramm | *Of the* |
| | Rev. Alfred Sutcliffe | *Primitive Methodist Church* |
| 1928 | Rev. G.H. Birch | Part Time Oversight |
| 1932 | Rev. Alfred Sutcliffe | |
| 1936 | Rev. Joseph Wellings | Supernumerary Minister |
| 1937 | Rev. G.H. Kennedy | Bournemouth Circuit |
| | Rev. John Bedford | Bournemouth Circuit |
| | Rev. T. Allerton | Bournemouth Circuit |
| 1940 | Rev. G. Hicks | Bournemouth Circuit |
| 1944 | Pastor Matthew Hill | Home Mission Appointment |
| 1946 | Rev. John Bedford | Supernumerary Minister |
| 1951 | Rev. Alfred Olds | Part Time Minister |

| | | |
|---|---|---|
| 1951 | Rev. Thomas Jukes | Supernumerary Minister |
| 1954 | Rev. John Myer | First Full Time Minister |
| 1958 | Rev. Gregory Carter | |
| 1963 | Rev. Sidney Fittall, B.D. | |
| 1968 | Rev. Roland Wilson, M.A., M.Th | |
| 1973 | Rev. G. Clifford Hunt | |
| 1981 | Rev. David Laidler | |
| 1991 | Rev. Royston Putnam | |
| 1992 | Rev. John Whitehurst, M.A. | American Probation Minister |
| 1993 | Rev. Philip Morse, B.A. | |
| 1995 | Rev. John Stanbury, M.A. | |
| 2002 | Rev. Robert Manning, M. Th. | |

## ROMAN CATHOLIC CHURCH

*Priests*

| | |
|---|---|
| Father Norman Fisher | 1965-1974 |
| Father Grundy | 1974-1998 |
| Father David Quarmby | 1998- |

# APPENDIX B

# General Practitioners Practising in Highcliffe

*I am indebted to the local doctors who, speaking from memory, have given the following information.*

| | | | |
|---|---|---|---|
| Dr. Hartford in Christchurch | | Dr. John Pillenger | 1986- |
| Dr. Deane in Christchurch | | Dr. Reginald Ogbert | 1990- |
| Dr. Busteed in Highcliffe | 1908 | Dr. Stephen Collins | 1992 |
| Dr. Marshall | 1914-1920 | Dr. Joanne Lee | 1992- |
| Dr. Howlett *(died whilst* | 1928-1940 | Dr. Naveed Sami | 2000- |
| *still a young man)* | | Dr. Lucy Godwin | 2001- |
| Dr. Bell | Late 1920's | Dr. Anne Lloyd Thomas | 2001- |
| Dr. Blood | 1930-1938 | | |
| Dr. Parker Williams | 1938-1964 | *Clinical Assistants:* | |
| Dr. Carr | 1946-1957 | | |
| Dr. Falkner-Lee | 1957-1989 | Dr. Eustasia Chritchley | 1995 |
| Dr. Brooks | 1960- | Dr. Cornelia Krasser | 2001-02 |
| Dr. Harcourt Webster | 1964 | Dr. Cheng | 2002- |
| Dr. Stevenson | 1969-1970 | | |
| Dr. Gilbertson | 1970-2001 | Dr. Barnett had his own | 1960-? |
| Dr. Pocock | 1978 | practice in Hinton Wood | |
| | | Avenue | |
| Dr. Scott | 1979 | | |

# APPENDIX C

## Staff of St. Mark's Church of England School

| *Appointed* | | | *Retired* |
|---|---|---|---|
| 1844 | Miss Belbin | | |
| 1867 | John Palmer | | |
| | Alfred Austin | | |
| 1873 | John Marston Turner | | |
| 1880 | Johnson | | |
| 1882 | Horatio Ellwood | Head | 1922 |
| 1888 | Miss Mary Anne Groves | | |
| | Miss Christiana Carey | | |
| 1889 | Miss Emily Vicary | | |
| 1890 | Miss Alice Wormington | | |
| | Miss Alice Greggs Tingey | | |
| 1891 | Miss Nellie White | | |
| | Miss Helen Sophia Bull | | |
| | Miss Marion Sheers | | |
| 1897 | Miss Jane Bartlett | | |
| | Miss Jane Mary Ginsburg | | |
| 1898 | Miss Parish | | 1903 |
| 1902 | Miss Dunn | | 1903 |
| 1903 | Miss Harvey | | 1903 |
| | Miss Cousins | | 1903 |
| | Miss Collings | | 1913 |
| 1905 | Miss Kellick | | 1906 |
| 1910 | Miss Phillips | | 1923 |
| | Miss Lawrence | | 1910 |
| 1911 | Miss Ferrett | | 1917 |
| 1913 | Miss Huray | | 1916 |
| 1914 | William Brown | | 1916 |
| 1919 | Miss Astridge | | 1959 |
| 1921 | Miss Edmunds | | 1927 |
| 1923 | Luther W. Newby Stubbs | Head | 1932 |
| 1923 | Miss Quelch | Head 1937 | Retired 1960 |
| 1932 | Frederick William Dyson | Head | 1937 |
| 1938 | Miss Morris | | 1943 |
| 1943 | Mrs. Gee | | 1943 |
| 1943 | Mrs. Freeman | | 1947 |

| 1945 | Mrs. Cruise | 1946 |
| 1946 | Miss Adams (Mrs. Crow) | 1948 |
| 1947 | Mrs. Primmer | 1947 |
|  | Miss Robinson | 1962 |
| 1948 | Mrs. Luff | 1952 |
| 1950 | Mrs. Smith | 1951 |
| 1951 | Miss Giles | 1970 |
| 1952 | Mr. Bateman (died) |  |
|  | Miss Knight | 1959 |
|  | Mr. Donald Hibberd | 1956 |
| 1954 | Miss Rogers | 1956 |
| 1956 | Mrs. Crow |  |
| 1957 | Mrs. Wakeford |  |
|  | Albert Stones |  |

# Staff of Highcliffe Junior School

| *Headmasters* | *Period of Office* |
| --- | --- |
| Robert Chacksfield | 1962-1977 |
| David Grainger | 1977- |
| John Warne B.A., Dip Ed. | |

| *Staff* | |
| --- | --- |
| A.E. Stones | 1962-1971 |
| Mrs. N.F. James | 1962-1969 |
| F.V.R. Field | 1962-1972 |
| Mrs. L.A. Wakefield | 1962-1971 |
| Miss G. Belcher | 1962-1963 |
| Miss J. Inger | 1962-1966 |
| Miss J. Thornton | 1962-1973 |
| A.W. Hyde | 1963-1963 |
| J.H. Sharpe | 1964-1965 |
| B.D. Webb | 1964-1968 |
| T.M. Richards | 1965-1965 |
| Mrs. E.A. Holmes | 1965-1966 |
| J.E. Blum | 1966-1971 |
| D.A. Eels | 1966- |
| Miss E. Neely | 1966-1969 |
| Mrs. G. Pitt | 1966-1968 |

I am indebted to Mr. John Warne for updating the following staff

Joan Lucas
Joan Roberts
George Tublin
Pauline Mueller
Susan Woodhouse
Mike Maddor
Shirley Scheslinger
Alison Chopping
Jackie Broomfield
Cathy Kirkham
Jackie Good
Ros Ortu
Fiona Cross
Fiona Thomas
Carol Rampley
Gill Honey
Julia Beehag
Joanna Watkins

| | | |
|---|---|---|
| Miss M. Denniss | 1967- | Myra Graham |
| Miss L. Potter | 1967-1969 | Emma Scott |
| Mrs. C.A. Pfaff | 1968-1969 | Eileen Ireland |
| J. Webber | 1968-1972 | Julia Whiteman |
| Mrs. D. Sheldon | 1968-1969 | Barbara Jeffries |
| Miss G. Garrett | 1969-1984 | Liz Corkell |
| Miss J. Knight | 1969-1975 | Wendy … |
| Mrs. P. Harvey | 1969- | Chris Baker |
| Miss I. Austin | 1970-1981 | Jan Randall |
| Miss V. Hewitt | 1971-1973 | Alson Craddock |
| H. Roderick | 1971- | Gill Jolliffe |
| Mrs. A. Clark | 1971- | Izzy Devall |
| Mrs. M. Graham | 1972-1973 | Jane Murray |
| Mrs. A. Herbert | 1972-1974 | Rosie Chandler |
| Mrs. E. Mason | 1973-1978 | Julia Hughes |
| P. Young | 1973-1974 | Howard Lovell |
| Mrs. S. Herringshaw | 1974-1984 | Lucy Webb |
| Mrs. M. Cooper | 1974-1976 | Louise Gray |
| Mrs. Jarvis | 1974-1975 | Rachel Ackroyd |
| Miss Sands | 1974-1975 | Gill Wilson |
| R. Dalziel | 1974-1978 | Tony Rogers |
| Mrs. G. Pitt | 1975- | Viv Buck |
| Mrs. Prosser | 1976-1977 | Hilary Bond |
| Mrs. J. Barrett | 1979- | Sarah Hill |
| Mrs. H. Wakefield | 1979- | |

# APPENDIX D

## Road Names

**Abingdon Drive**
The Earl of Abingdon married Elizabeth, daughter of Major General Stuart Wortley.

**Amberwood Drive**
**Amberwood Gardens**
} Part of the Amberwood Estate

**Balfour Close**
Maud Edith Balfour was the sister of Gen. Browne of Hoburne in whose memory the Red Cross Medical Hut was built.

**Beacon Drive**
Part of the Beacon lodge estate

**Bure Land**
**Bure Homage Lane**
**Bure Homage Gardens**
**Bure Road**
} These were all part of the Bure Homage Estate

**Castle Avenue**
This road leads to the Castle

**Chewton Common Road**
**Chewton Farm Road**
**Chewton Way**
} The villages of Chewton Common and Chewton

**Cranemoor Avenue**
**Cranemoor Close**
**Cranemoor Gardens**
} Cranemoor Estate

**Curzon Way**
Lord and Lady Curzon Howe lived at Hoburne and leased Highcliffe Castle.

**Elphinstone Road**
May be named after T.P. Elphinstone who lived at Cranemoor or the Elphinstone family who once lived at Field Place.

**Gordon Road**
After General Gordon of Khartoum.

**Hinton Wood Avenue**
A rhododendron walk through woods to Hinton – known also as Station Road and where it joins Castle Avenue as Ice House Hill.

**Hoburne Gardens**
**Hoburne Lane**
} Hoburne Estate

**Holmhurst Avenue**
Holmhurst Estate

**Latimers Close**
After the old house of Latimers.

**Loraine Avenue**
Sir Percy married Louise, daughter of General Stuart Wortley.

**Mill Lane**
Leads to Mill House.

**Montagu Road**
Edward Montagu Wortley, and ancestor of the owners of the Castle.

| | |
|---|---|
| **Nada Road** | Named after Gen. Browne's favourite horse. |
| **Nea Close**<br>**Nea Road** | } Nea Estate |
| **Rothesay Drive** | Lord Stuart de Rothesay who built Highcliffe Castle. |
| **St. George's Close** | St. George's School previously stood on the site. |
| **Saulflands Drive**<br>**Saulflands Place**<br>**Saulflands House** | } From the original Saxon owner of the site, Saulf. |
| **Shelley Close** | Shelley Hill, the house owned by Edward Huntley Hooper. |
| **Shepherd Close** | Mr. and Mrs. Shepherd were the gardener and lodge keeper to the Holmhurst estate. |
| **Smugglers Lane**<br>**Smugglers Wood Road** | } A path used by smugglers. |
| **Stuart Road** | The owners of the Castle – Stuart Wortleys. |
| **Studley Close** | John Studley – farmer of Chewton Farm. |
| **Thursby Road** | Sir John Thursby lived on the Holmhurst estate on which the road was built. |
| **Waterford Gardens** | Louisa, daughter of Lord Stuart de Rothesay, married the Marquis of Waterford. |
| **Wellington Avenue** | The Duke of Wellington appointed Lord Stuart de Rothesay as British Ambassador in Paris. |
| **Wharncliffe Gardens**<br>**Wharncliffe Road** | } Baron Wharncliffe, ancestor of the Stuart Wortleys |
| **Wingfield Avenue** | After the house called Wingfield which stood on the site. |
| **Wortley Road** | Stuart Wortleys were owners of the Castle. |

*To the native of Highcliffe the following names are familiar:*

| | |
|---|---|
| **Froggy Lane** | The footpath from the Walkford Hotel to the Milestone. |
| **Bloods Corner** | Named after Dr. Blood who lived on the corner of Lymington Road and Chewton Common Road. |

# BIBLIOGRAPHY

The School Logs – by courtesy of Mr. Grainger and Mrs. Little

*The Stuarts of Highcliffe* by Robert Franklin

*Highcliffe Castle* by Tahu Hole

*Highcliffe Castle* by Henry Salsbury

*The Ancient Estate of Nea*
*Hoburne*              } by Olive J. Samuel
*Saulflands*

The Parish Magazines of St. Mark's Church – by courtesy of the Rev. J. Seaford

*Life without Theory*
*Magic in the Distance*   } by Mrs. Violet Stuart Wortley
*Grow Old Along with Me*